SENIORHOOD ISN'T FOR SISSIES

Conceived and edited by Cynthia MacGregor

Acknowledgments

Thanks to Michael Sharpe for allowing this book to see the light of print so easily.

Thanks to all the contributors who shared their stories for the book.

Dedication

To all my friends who are facing the same pitfalls, perils, and rigors of seniorhood, whether they are just entering this phase (hello, Mari!) Or looking back from a more advanced point on the age spectrum (hello Shirl!).

SENIORHOOD ISN'T FOR SISSIES

Conceived and edited by Cynthia MacGregor

Michele Sharpe, Executive Publisher
AcuteByDesign
Marlborough, Connecticut
https://www.acutebydesign.com
ISBN: 978-1-943515-19-6
©2019 Cynthia MacGregor

AcuteByDesign
the little book company that could
A Michael Marion Sharpe Company

Cover Artwork - Sanghamitra Dasgupta
Book Layout - Meg Petrillo

Contents

Introduction

Senior Dis-Counts, by Lorraine Harrison — 1

The Grim Reaper Apparently Drives a Pickup Truck, by Mark T. Holmes — 3

Everything You Wanted to Know About Dating After Sixty, but Were Afraid to Ask, by Beverly Lessard — 15

Water, Water Everywhere, by Bess W. Metcalf — 19

The Tea, by Ann Favreau — 23

Harry Up, by Bobbie Christmas — 27

My Sleep Apnea Test, by Linda Parsons — 37

Second Marriage...or Not? by Iris E. Price — 41

Ghost Train, by John Sheffield — 49

Hurrah for Subtitles, by Beverly Lessard — 55

A Few Quickies from the ALF, by Lenna Buissink — 59

Crooked Toes, by Deborah Robinson — 63

Getting It Done in Florida, by Margaret Jane Jones — 67

Downsizing, by Lorraine Harrison — 69

Contents

Passing Myself on the Stairs: ADD Got the Better of Me, by Sharon Love Cook	73
Cellphonin' It In, by Mark Daponte	77
We'd Better Not Get Married, by Cynthia MacGregor	79
Old Is a Word, by Bob Lebensold	87
Who Ever Heard of a Senior Standup Comic? by Sharon Love Cook	91
There Are Crazies Swimming in the Senior Dating Pool, by Arthur Lindower	95
Bees in the Bonnet and Birds Among the Hats, by Erika Hoffman	99
OMG, SMH, and IDGAF, by Mark T. Holmes	105
Across the Vast Divide, by Ann Favreau	115
A Day in the Life, by Linda Peters	119
Looking Back from Ninety-One, by Dan Samuelson	125
Cleavage Connection, by Bobbie Christmas	129

Introduction

There's a meme going around Facebook that proclaims OLD AGE AIN'T FOR SISSIES. I agree, but I would like to propose that old age doesn't start till you're consigned to the nursing home, or your spouse or Significant Other is spending so much time taking care of you that their friends have forgotten what they look like.

Prior to that, you're not old; you're merely a senior.

But seniorhood isn't for sissies either.

I have a friend who's a talented artist who is ninety-one years old. She turns out new paintings with amazing frequency. She insists that she doesn't live alone: her dog is her faithful companion. But if you don't count her dog, she's living on her own. So at ninety-one is she "old"? Not by my standards! She's certainly a senior, but she does live alone (despite what she says about her dog, Sophie can't vacuum her floors or do her laundry, play Scrabble™ with her, argue politics with her, or call 911 in a health emergency), and working on her art every day, and swimming daily at the Y, Shirl is not, I aver, old.

But she recently suffered two broken arms—one at a time. Her dog couldn't cook for her, help her get dressed with only one functioning arm, or do her painting for her— and it was her dominant arm that she broke.

But Shirl got through it. Seniorhood isn't for sissies, but I'm here to tell you Shirl is no sissy—and she proved it. She also proved that, even at ninety-one, she's not old!

Nearly ten years ago I went to visit my daughter and grandkids. There was a tall, fortlike playhouse in the back yard. My youngest grandson was playing in it. I climbed up to join him and, after a bit, I returned to the ground via the slide that extended down from the fort to ground level. CRUNCH! CRACK! When I landed, I broke both bones in my right ankle.

I was in a cast in a wheelchair for five weeks. My S.O. took excellent care of me, but I developed a UTI and had to pee several times a night. I had to wake up my poor suffering S.O. to wheel me to the bathroom every time. Since cooking was somewhere between difficult and impossible for me in the wheelchair, and since cooking is not in Grant's skill set, we ate a lot of take-out for those five weeks. The Chinese restaurant must have hung black crepe and gone into mourning when I finally was permitted to stand up and put weight on my leg, and I was able to cook again.

But after all that, Grant suggested strongly that "Nanas shouldn't slide down slides." And I am sure I won't anymore. I certainly don't want to go through *that* again!

When I was younger (but already an adult), I slid down slides. Long, long ago, when I was preggers, I slid down a playground slide—to the utter horror and disbelief of my neighbors. Neither my daughter-in-development nor I suffered any ill effects. But since the ankle travesty, while slides maintain their allure, I give them a wide berth. Seniorhood isn't for sissies.

But if I can still *climb up the ladder* of the slide, even if I don't dare slide down. I haven't yet reached old age.

Take that, actuaries!

Senior Dis-Counts
Lorraine Harrison

It started with the ubiquitous, "May I help you out with your groceries, ma'am?" *Ma'am?* It was like getting slapped in the face with a dead fish. Then came the invitation to join AARP. That was enough to cause previously happy blonde hair follicles to consider going gray.

It didn't take long before gray became a reality. Thank goodness for hair color. I wasn't doing this by myself. My husband's dark eyebrows, sideburns, and goatee were displaying a smattering of white. Using hair color for men, he left the dye on too long. It made him look like Beelzebub.

We had to either ban mirrors from the house or hit the gym. Fab arms became flab arms. Waving now involved the entire appendage, from fingertips to armpits. I blame gravity.

Next came senior discounts. All of a sudden, movie tickets were less than general admission prices. The urge to ask the twelve-year-old behind the counter, "How old do you think I am?" was strong but successfully suppressed. It's a two-way street. I saw a kid driving a car just a few weeks later and started to laugh, thinking he must have just gotten his driver's license. Then I noticed he was driving a police car. I might look older, but "kids" has become a wider category, and they look younger and younger.

After thirty-eight years at one company, my husband retired. We said good-bye to

Colorado winters and hello to the Sunshine State. In order to be as cliché as possible, we bought a boat and unapologetically named it *The Cliché*. It's important to use clear labels as the memory starts to slip.

Our world changed. All around us were people our age or older. Our daughter came to visit. We went out night fishing. When we came back, there was a band playing and people dancing in the parking lot. She was surprised to see so many old folks partying it up, asking, "Is this what goes on around here?" We've sworn her to silence on the subject.

Aging takes some getting used to. Everything takes a little longer. Some of the new technology works better if you're on the other side of sixty. It's true that it's not for wimps.

Meanwhile, it's three in the afternoon. Time for dinner!

* * *

Like many before them, Lorraine and her husband retired and moved to the Sunshine State. They bought a boat ('The Cliché') and fish in the Gulf. Her husband, "MacGyver," is a retired chemist. Now he's the neighborhood's unconventional Mr. Fix-it. Lorraine's career was in marketing. Now she's a part-time writer. Her first novel, *Grip of Change*, is available on Amazon. A collection of short stories and a second novel are in the works.

The Grim Reaper Apparently Drives a Pickup Truck
Mark T. Holmes

It started the day I found a one-inch hair growing out of the middle of my forehead; yes, the geographic center of the cranial area above my nose. I shuddered. I was then thankful that I was the one who'd found it, and not Paul over at the barber shop. Oh, he'd quietly and discreetly snip it off without comment while politely stifling a chuckle, but I'd have known what he was up to, and deeper into the leather chair I'd sink. So at least I'm thankful for that. I'm used to Paul casually trimming ear hair while he dodges skillfully around my skull with those expensive scissors, but the ignominy of having him pluck that strand would have been a very new low in my rapidly advancing seniorhood.

That hair, that singular banner of oldness, defines a new era for me. It's one that surpasses even the moment I caught myself turning halfway with my entire body and my mouth wide open in oldster curiosity to ponder something that caught my eye. Oh sure, I've been dealing with other foibles of older age like an annoying little single hair that frequently appears on top of my nose, the same kind I used to stare at on the bulbous nose of my former coworker, or even the odd one that I found one day exiting the side of one nostril. No, it was the long, flowing one exploding out of my forehead that certified the first sign of certain doom. The grim reaper has started his engine, and I think I hear it rumbling behind the gas station. Oh, dear.

    Aging is very entertaining if you have an open mind and practical joker's sense of humor. For example, I now have a new set of decisions to make such as when I drop something on the floor and then take a moment to decide if it's worth picking up. In that same realm, my new best friend forever is my grabber stick from Home Depot. With careful aim and a squeeze of the handle, this thing picks up a dime, and that's a good thing because I collect them. Not because I admire tiny, shiny portraits of FDR, but because once I have enough of them, I take them in a bag over to Publix (our supermarket) and drop them in the change machine. It spits out a receipt that I can exchange for real cash money, not like that annoying plastic cup of grimy change I keep next to my keys. You know, the cup I got at the casino the night they had one-dollar draft beer.

    I no longer count days; I count Fridays instead. Like tonight is Thursday and tomorrow it's another Friday and that means dragging the 96-gallon trash containers out to the curb, plus the more petite blue recycling container as well. They must be placed just so—not too far in the swale and not too far on the pavement. Heaven forbid a waste management professional would have to get out of his truck. I can distinctly remember, when I was a kid, the Adonis-like garbageman stalking through our yard purposefully, lifting the galvanized can up to his shoulder, and carrying that thing out to the truck, a good 75 feet away. To him it was nothing. If I had to do it today, it would cost me a small fortune in payoffs to the neighbor's kid. Another reason to pick up those dimes. But anyway, time flies so fast these days, you need a swivel chair to keep up. So, it's easier to just count Fridays, and in fact, I once calculated approximately how many Fridays I probably had left this side of the turf. It was disheartening. but being the sometime optimist I am, the notion quickly passed.

    I'm semi-retired, which means I still work, but I work for myself, so I don't have to politely smile at blithering idiots who run other company departments while sucking up to the CEO and trying to undermine my best efforts with the other hand. I *am* the CEO of my own S-corporation, and when I want to take a day off, I just do it. Of course, the real reason I'm such an entrepreneur is that I got laid off ten years ago at age fifty-seven, and when you're in marketing, your staff lovingly refers to you as *"gringo viejo"* and you don't really speak Spanish in South Florida, *and* the economy is tanking like it's

1929...well, you end up working for yourself. As my good buddy Don, a PR professional, told me, "Mark, they're not looking for a guy like you. They want a perky thirty-five-year-old." Despite being rock-solid-certain that age discrimination does not exist in the workplace—*ahem*—I rather believed the man.

And what exactly does a mid-fifties man who speaks only enough Spanish to order dinner at La Carreta do with himself? Of course! He has lunch or coffee with everyone he knows to pluck their brains for job leads. Oh, did I mention the economy had tanked? Nobody was hiring an old *gringo* in the marketing field in South Florida when there were perky thirty-five-year-olds with advanced degrees, dazzling artificially whitened teeth, and falsified resumes lined up for every position. But I did have some fun catching up with people who uncomfortably told me they'd be on the lookout for something for me.

Folks, I continue to wait for your promised leads. Still, liking to eat, and having a daughter with two horses to feed, shoe, and house, I became the reluctant entrepreneur, putting up my virtual shingle and pawning stuff to pay the vet bills.

Ten years later, my company is still in business although my accountant daughter-in-law secretly smirks when she forwards me my Schedule K-1. There's not a whole lot of profit to pass through to my personal tax return, but I work in Kahala shorts, Ralph Lauren Polo t-shirts, and my ever-present OluKai sandals. I own long pants and shirts with buttons, but I'm not sure where they are. I somehow manage to scrape together enough regular-people clothes to make me presentable on dress-up night aboard one of the Holland America ships, but damn those shoes with laces!

Balancing having enough water to stay healthfully hydrated and not drinking so much I wake up twice at night is a twisted hobby I've embraced. Remembering to down enough H2O is the first challenge, and—*news flash*—you can't forget all day then make up for it at 8 PM and expect a child-like sleep. So I keep a large pitcher of filtered tepid water in plain view in the kitchen to remind me that Dr. Oz and everyone else wants me hydrated.

Fine. I'm hydrated—if only that were the least of my worries. In plain fact, we all have our hurdles to overcome and our own crosses to bear, and I'm not one for bitching and moaning about mine, knowing full well there are plenty of other Boomers with plenty more problems. So, I'm not going there. You have yours; I have mine. I wish you well in combating your set of woes, and I hope you do the same for me. Life's too short and getting shorter. As Dickens noted, we're all fellow passengers to the grave. Some of us sooner than others. To wit:

My own dad passed at age fifty-eight. You'd say, "He was so young!" but in fact he wasn't. Dad was a bomber pilot in World War II and flew through such horror, I cannot imagine. He had a desk job after the war and got zero exercise other than opening a new Four Roses bottle or a pack of Chesterfields, and so when a visit from AMI came one night, he simply did not wake up. Those acute myocardial infarcts are a bitch, but at least you go fast. A few years earlier, his seventy-two-year-old dad, my grandpa, had his own AMI standing at the edge of a lake, fishing. Boom! Fell dead on the spot.

Thinking back to a happy time, I can vividly recall the three of us sitting in a rowboat, silently fishing for bass or pickerel. Fishing and going to Yankees games were the ties that bound us. That both my dad and grandpa keeled over quickly gives me hope for the rapidity of my own eventual demise, but I don't smoke while they both did, nor do I drink much. I wonder if I'm robbing myself of the ultimate E-ticket trip out of here.

I still have most of my driving skills, or at least I've convinced myself that I do, but night vision is quite another subject. Yes, the windows on my Outback are tinted, which is damned helpful in the Florida sun but a dark curse at night. So I put both front windows down when backing up at night in hopes of seeing any oncoming cars or the neighbor down the street walking Bailey, his energetic

Yorkie. I don't want to squish cute Bailey, and especially his owner, who happens to be an attorney with the license plate LITIJUS, or something similarly forbidding.

    Not having to commute to work beyond the casual stroll from my kitchen to my home office has made me a languid driver, and that annoys ninety percent of the other drivers out there, who seem hellishly preoccupied with getting to the next red light before me, dammit. I don't purposefully annoy them, but I don't play the game anymore, either. I do, however, appreciate the safety features on my newer Subaru Outback, especially the rear-view camera that beeps if someone is coming across behind me. After my nursing fourteen years out of my Isuzu Trooper, the guys at the Subaru dealer just laughed when I came to trade it in. I really liked the Trooper, but enough was enough. I do, however, love my Subaru, just like the ad says.

    The drivers who amuse me the most are the ones with the big-tire pickups, exhaust pipes the size of a small pine tree trunk, and about four feet of ground clearance. At speed, the knobby tires sound like an F-14 Tomcat taking off from the USS *Eisenhower*—on their way, of course, to the vitamin store or gym, where they so purposefully and slowly stride across the parking lot, bulging arms sticking out from tank-tops while intently studying their smartphones, earbuds in place and carrying a gallon jug of purified water. I once asked my wife what kind of man drives such a truck, and her answer was, "A guy with a one-inch dick." God bless her heart.

Jack Nicholson and Morgan Freeman had their bucket lists, and I have mine, albeit a much shorter one. My list included writing something worth reading. I've written a few books and found it to be oddly cathartic and fun. The first was, in hindsight, a truly insipid book of poetry composed of many thirty- and forty-year-old poems I'd written under various personal influences. I don't even promote it anymore. The yellow pad on which these crudely composed poems were written was dog-eared and worn, but since I'd kept it all these years, I wanted to make a complete work. Not all of what I wrote impressed me years later. In fact, a fair amount made me wonder just exactly what I had eaten to cause such a vomitous tome to spring forth from my hand.

That meant writing some new stuff to fill in. I found inspiration from the rain, from the wind chimes outside my front door, and from my dog. I thought back to other formative events in my life and before long had eighty pages of "stuff" suitable to make a respectably thick-enough paperback. A few hours on Amazon's CreateSpace and I was ready to go, using my own cover photo of a North Carolina stream and the title, *Streams to Ford*. I liked it at the time and even cajoled a few family members and friends—or probably now former friends—to buy copies. I can't remember the last time one sold online. Five years later, I think less of it, to be quite honest but one of those recent poems I wrote appeals to me, and so I'll share it:

> *Taken one drop at a time*
> *Today's hard rain seems no match for me*
> *But the creek just past the tree line*
> *Is starting to rise, and with it*
> *My suspicions...*
> *Will I stick to my plan of work so thoroughly*
> *Crafted the night before?*
> *Or will I leave the keyboard for the forest*
> *Pine cones to be captured*
> *Rocks to be overturned*
> *And streams to ford*

Briefly aglow with the relative success of putting my words to print, I went to work on my second book, a real one this time, harkening on my somewhat rowdy past as a Coast Guardsman in the 1970s. This one came pretty easy, written from a fading memory of scurrilous events and rescues at sea, helped along by a few of my former shipmates, whom I found on Facebook or had been in contact with ever since the early '70s. Called *Always Ready—Coast Guard Sea Stories From the 1970s*, with the tag line, "Radios, Rescues, & Rowdiness," it was published on Amazon in 2015 and, with my

USCG contacts to help, has sold quite a few copies, paying enough royalties to enjoy dinner a number of times at restaurants where the lady's menu shows no prices.

My third book was a literary shout-out to my dad, the B-24 pilot who died too young. Since nearly everyone wrote their books about their father's actual war experiences, instead of sticking my finger down that throat, I elected to take a different route, borrowing a lot from his actual mission log, but twisting one mission where he crash-landed into a spy story. The book practically wrote itself, and it flowed from me like I was reading the novel instead of writing it, wondering where the story would go next and wondering who that "adventurous" female British spy would bed next . It's called *Artifact—A B-24 Crew, a British Spy, and Churchill's Deadly Obsession.*

I'm telling you all this not so you'll go find the books and buy them, but to encourage you to go ahead and write *your* book. Buy mine if you insist on seeing how I did it. *Ahem.* It's not as difficult as you may think. You begin simply, by beginning.

I'm not a curmudgeon *per se*, but I did stay at a Holiday Inn Express, so that gives me the opportunity to opine regarding foolish spending by the city council, weighing in on Facebook subjects that I don't actually care about, and erasing half of the wise-ass comments I truly want to say but withhold, keeping in mind the adage, "If you have nothing nice to say, then say nothing at all." I do have a "no soliciting" sticker near my doorbell because no, I don't want to buy a magazine subscription so you can attend a convention of magazine sellers in Poughkeepsie, have my lawn treated with a brew of fertilizer and weed-killing chemicals, or have my windows replaced. I can still do my own pressure-washing, I am perfectly happy with my Internet service; yes, I know Jesus, and no, I don't want your clever little LDS handout, but thanks for interrupting my football game.

    Okay, I'm a curmudgeon, but I still give a few bucks to the kids at the grocery store begging for help "going to State," whatever that is, and I'll send a nice check or make an online donation to Americares or Food for the Poor. Both agencies do great work with very low overhead. And, in my tender older age, I'm okay with just enjoying a perfect morning with low humidity, watching kids play over at the park, holding my wife's hand, and savoring a great meal at a friendly but overpriced restaurant. If I have the ability to remember anything after crossing the bar (as we Coast Guardsmen like to say), I hope to remember things such as these. Maybe we'll run into each other. I'll be the guy wearing Kahala shorts.

* * *

Mark T. Holmes is a commercial writer and former marketing executive for large banks and credit unions. Following a layoff from a lucrative senior marketing job at one of the nation's largest credit unions during the past recession, Mr. Holmes formed his own Florida S-corporation, Idea Depot, Inc., and began writing high-end military transition and executive federal resumes, along with doing web development and optimization work gaining page one results, plus marketing writing for a message-on-hold company.

In 2014, Mr. Holmes released his first book, *Streams to Ford*, a book of poetry long in the making, followed in 2015 by *Always Ready—Coast Guard Sea Stories from the 1970s*," and in 2016, the World War II novel *Artifact—A B-24 Crew, a British Spy, and Churchill's Deadly Obsession*. All books are available in print and Kindle format on Amazon.

Mark and his wife, Sheri, operate a retail location in an antique mall and trade in antiques and vintage cameras in the store and online.

Everything You Wanted to Know About Dating After Sixty, but Were Afraid to Ask
Beverly Lessard

The person who said you have to break a few eggs to make an omelet obviously had not entered the world of "over-sixty" online dating. After a month, I had a trashcan full of eggshells and my soufflé had blown up in the oven.

It all started innocently enough when the thirtysomething son of a friend suggested online dating as a way to meet a few men. My husband had passed away the previous year and, if nothing else, I might find someone to golf with or at least a dinner companion.

Sounded good—right? And it did—at least on paper.

As I prepared for my first date, searching for an outfit that fit and didn't have any paint stains on it, I had no idea the education I was about to receive.

To start with, I discovered that my prospective dates no longer resembled the rambunctious lads of my early dating years.

Not that I wanted a teenage boy, but the men over sixty looked like they should be dating my grandmother, not me. And yet, this was my age group. This was going to be a tough journey, I thought, trying not to cringe as I scrolled down the page of the online potentials.

But just as I was feeling way too young for these men, I began to see that in many respects they hadn't aged either. It soon became obvious that the only difference between a sixty-year-old man and a sixteen-year-old boy was some crow's feet, a few extra pounds, and a few gray hairs. Sixty-year-old men may have calmed down a bit while perfecting their courting style, but deep down they haven't changed a bit.

Not surprisingly, I found that people over sixty had become more focused on who they were and what they wanted. While that isn't a bad thing, it significantly cuts down the odds of meeting one's soulmate. With my own long laundry list of likes and dislikes, finding the person who might share my interests soon looked more like mission impossible.

While I consider myself broad minded, with tons of interests, I was amazed to find so many things in life that are of no interest. For example, sitting in a restaurant listening to my date's top twenty fishing stories made my eyes roll almost out of my head. Another date's two-hour monologue on his annual ski weekends had me holding my keys waiting for him to stop talking long enough so I could say goodnight and sprint out the door.

Dating was definitely easier as a teenager, when we rarely held long conversations, and our number-one criterion was how we looked.

I also discovered that most men in their sixties no longer remembered how to give the soft, innocent kisses they stole as a youth. The new, experienced dating seniors have practiced way too many years to settle for a soft peck on the cheek. And while a long, warm kiss is very nice, I prefer to know my date's last name before I become lip-locked.

Batting zero after the first several dates, I began to wonder about the man's point of view. So I made a perfectly happy guy friend sign up, too. He emerged totally perplexed after finding sixty-year-old women much more aggressive and demanding than they had been in high school. My friend's voice shook in disbelief as he relayed the responses he was getting. One date posted on her profile that she looked fabulous in high heels and nothing else.

Each night, he faithfully reported back his data, hoping it was enough and that I'd leave him alone. After all, he hadn't even had his third date and was out almost $300.

"Enough," he said one day. "I can't afford this anymore.

On the other hand, I was enjoying the fact that guys still pay. While I tried not to take advantage of their generosity, it was nice to leave the credit card at home while selecting off the part of the menu marked, "market value to be determined after you order." To be honest, I did feel guilty, but who am I to question the system?

And besides, it was nice to find that men were still charming and complimentary. They still opened car doors and told their dates how nice they looked.

And it was lovely to find men who wore their hearts on their sleeves, unlike their younger selves, and were able to talk about their life experiences and what made them happy.

And even though I'm no longer looking for the eager young male I once found so exciting, I have to admit that behind the age-embossed faces of my over-sixty dates, there seem to lurk the heart and soul of the forever young.

* * *

Beverly Lessard is the author of several humorous books including *Relentlessly Upbeat* and *Knee Deep in Sawdust and Fudge Brownie Mix*, and one serious one: *Are You Emotionally Ready to Retire?* A New England resident, she is a mother and proud grandma, loves to write, and particularly enjoys golf.

Water, Water Everywhere
Bess W. Metcalf

Maybe you'll find some humor in this. I hope so. We really didn't!

Last Thursday, as I write this, when I started to wash my hands in the lavatory, the water wouldn't turn off! I finally got it stopped after several tries and called the plumber, who said he was booked solid and would come Friday afternoon.

Well, Friday I woke before dawn with the "stomach flu"—at both ends! So absent-mindedly I started to wash my hands—and the darn cold-water faucet actually exploded. Water was hitting the ceiling and spraying all over the entire bathroom. I couldn't do anything about it; if I got down on the floor to close the cut-off valve, I wouldn't be able to get up. (I'm a bit crippled due to my post-polio syndrome, which came on about thirty-five years ago.)

So, totally nude and dripping, I ran out and banged on my daughter's bedroom door. Naturally she thought it was an emergency and ran out, also starkers, to find an actual fountain in the bathroom. I threw something over the faucet, which stopped it enough that we could see.

At my instruction, Cathy got down on all fours and tried to turn off the cut-off valve in a cupboard beside the lavatory. It wouldn't turn! She put on a shift and went out back to my tool drawers to find a tool I asked for. No luck! I then managed to get on my knees, first tried by hand, then even tapped it with a small tack hammer. Nothing!

Finally Cathy got more properly dressed, got a rug to kneel on, and went outside to turn off the water to the entire house. She was a bit hysterical as now the toilets, sinks, and every appliance in the house that was dependent on water would have none. She could not find the tool I had asked her to look for.

When she got up a little later to get ready for work, I got up too, put on a shift, and went out to look for the tool—which, of course, was right where I'd said it was. I then got down on my knees and turned off the cold-water check valve, but the hot water wouldn't budge. Testing the lavatory faucets (carefully), I determined it was only the cold faucet that had turned into a fountain.

So Cathy, who is the soul of patience most of the time, got me up off the floor, went outside, and carefully turned on the house water a bit, waiting to see if I'd scream. Determining it was okay, she then finished turning the main cut-off valve. One problem: I knew it had come on because I heard the toilet filling. But we now had *no water*.

We finally figured it out: Cathy has been dyslexic all her life. She can't tell right from left, north from south, clockwise from counter-clockwise, and such. She finally learned to read well and mostly manages. But after turning the main faucet *on*, and waiting, she had then got her directions mixed up and turned it *off*.

Eventually we got it straightened out, she cleaned water off everything—even the ceiling!—and got to work late. I called the plumber and rescheduled for Saturday, and went back to bed.

I'd like to say that everything is fine, except the plumber had emergencies Saturday and got here late and exhausted. We have water, but he was too exhausted to change the cut-off valves, and we still have a big problem. My late husband, who never was all there when it came to renovations, had proudly brought back from a trip a beautiful used lavatory top he bought at his beloved sister's used furniture store. The problem? Someone had cut off the back. He insisted I use it in my renovations, and sometimes I had to go along to keep peace.

It's so short in back, it's almost impossible to install lavatory faucet sets. The plumber did his best and thought it was okay, but after he left we found it was leaking into the cabinet below. Cathy arranged an aluminum foil cookie pan with a drain to catch it, and I'm waiting until I feel like getting underneath with a flashlight to see if there's any way to alter the cabinet.

The same plumber (he was a bit younger and skinnier then) replaced the faucets a few years ago (I had to cut out part of a shelf), and it too had a leak, but just one drip every fifteen or twenty minutes. I put a pan under it, and after a few months it stopped leaking on its own.

I'm sure we won't be so lucky this time. I'm going to partially turn off the cold-water cut-off valve to have less leak while I decide what to do.

Oh, and I got over the crud by Sunday evening, so it's not all bad!

* * *

Bess W. Metcalf is a Fuller Brush and Stanley products distributor in Miami, Florida, and writes a weekly column for "EZine Does It." She publishes "The Sneaky Kitchen" newsletter, which is filled with recipes, stories, trivia—and information about Fuller Brush and Stanley products. Find it at http://sneakykitchen.com

The Tea
Ann Favreau

I never expected to belly laugh at a ladies' tea, but that is exactly what happened. In early December, my daughter AnnMarie and I drove to Crosley Estate in Sarasota, Florida to see the decorated trees and to have afternoon tea. The architecture of the building and the furnishings in the rooms were enhanced by multitudes of Christmas trees. Each was uniquely designed by area artists and featured real orchids and other tubed flowers, massive and tiny ornaments, and intricate origami animals. In the area filled with gingerbread houses, the aromas piqued our appetites, and the time soon arrived to enter the room set aside for the tea.

AnnMarie and I chose seats at a large round table that faced the window. The water on Sarasota Bay was whipped into whitecaps by the wind, and the sun glinted off the surface. As the other ladies entered, we wondered who would be sitting with us. Two women with English accents sat at AnnMarie's right. One sported an enormous white linen hat that sat low on her forehead, so we could not see her eyes. We introduced ourselves and tried to initiate conversation, but they were interested only in talking to one another. Then in walked a mother and daughter, who sat at my left.

The mother was a stunning elderly woman with white hair, beautiful skin, and a twinkle in her eye. Her daughter was an equally stylish woman with blonde hair cut in a unique way that flattered her face. As AnnMarie poured the tea into the china cups, the new ladies said hello and received the same cold shoulder from the other two that we had experienced. There was no option but to ignore their rude behavior and talk to one another.

    The huge hat triggered the conversation. The mother told us that she had worked in a boutique in Vermont that sold hats as well as clothing, lingerie, and accessories. I asked her how she got the job. She replied that she was just a teenager and went in to browse, and they offered her a position. I am sure that because she was a stunning beauty in her younger years, she was an asset to their business. As we munched on tiny sandwiches, scones, and calamondin bread, and refilled our tea cups over and over, we exchanged stories.

    The mother told us about her unusual eightieth birthday present. Her sons had made arrangements with her husband to take the whole family, including daughters, husbands, wives, and grandchildren to a lovely family breakfast. Following the meal, they drove around the neighborhood and pulled into the parking lot of an unquestionably unique place—a tattoo parlor. One son explained that his mother's casual remark to his wife that she had always wanted a tattoo but never got one because it was just not the thing to do when she was growing up had led them to suggest that now might be the right time. He said that it was her choice, and she didn't have to do it if she didn't want to. She was excited and eagerly agreed.

    The son had previously called the owner of the establishment to explain that they were cat people. He had preselected a variety of small cat tattoos for her perusal. She chose the outline of a black cat with green eyes and decided she wanted it applied to her butt. As she went on with her description, I put my hand over my mouth to stifle a laugh. In vivid detail she described lying on the table with her milky white cheeks peeking out of the towel as her whole family watched the tattoo artist apply the inks.

    AnnMarie and I couldn't help ourselves. We both let out a belly laugh that rocked the room. As we sat there convulsed, our narrator went on to say that it was such a thrill and didn't hurt too much. She explained that the cat had not gotten any fatter but had certainly grown taller. Again we howled with glee at the vision of the cat on her sagging behind. She revealed that this year on her eighty-third birthday, she planned to have a little mouse tattoo added, if they could find a piece of firm skin. By now, the whole room of ladies sharing tea looked around to ascertain why we were having such a hilarious time.

The hat lady and her friend at our table missed the best story of the day. We didn't care.

As we finished our tea and wished our new acquaintances a Merry Christmas, AnnMarie and I marveled at the resilience of this elderly woman. Surprisingly, the ladies from other tables stopped by to say that we were having too much fun and wished they had been sitting with us. It was an afternoon tea we will remember with delight.

* * *

Ann Favreau is a vibrant eighty-one-year-old retired educator, who lives in Venice, Florida. She is a member of the Florida Writers Association and past president of the Suncoast Writers Guild, Inc. Her writing has been published in many newspapers, magazines, anthologies, and ezines. She has won local and national prizes for her prose and poetry. She is a thirty-one-year colorectal cancer survivor and a member of the National Colorectal Cancer Roundtable. Her most recent book, *It's Okay to Have an Ostomy,* is available on Amazon.com. Currently she is president of the Friends of Ostomates Worldwide-USA, a national non-profit organization that sends donated ostomy supplies at no cost to ostomates in need in 90 countries around the world. She describes herself as a traveler who marvels at the awesome and finds wonder in the ordinary.

Harry Up
Bobbie Christmas

Senior dating isn't for sissies—that's for sure; but even in my seventies, I still stuck my toe in the waters of that shallow dating pool in hopes of finding a man who shared my interests. As a result I've had some interesting, odd, and funny dates. The one with Harry, as I'll call him, though, felt like one of the longest forty-five minutes in history.

Oh, for sure I had clues beforehand that the prospects weren't ideal, but determined to kiss every frog to find my prince, I ignored the signs. Harry contacted me through an online dating site, and while I didn't care for the macho identification he used on his profile, the gist of his lengthy, in-depth profile impressed me. He said, "I am a kind, caring, passionate, and independent thinker, in some ways not your typical man...the conversation has no limits," adding that he was "quite intuitive" and believed in abundancy. Abundancy is an issue I used to struggle with, before I accepted that there is an abundance of all that we need in life. His word choices made me think the guy might be someone with depth who leaned toward the metaphysical, as I do, so I responded to his brief first message to me.

We wrote back and forth awhile, although he wrote mostly one-liners, nothing like his extensive and lyrical profile. After only a few notes from him, I knew someone else had written his profile. Oh, well. I hoped the content was correct, anyway.

Time passed with one-liners from him almost every day, sometimes several a day, mostly simply saying, "Hi."

I asked him to write to me through my regular e-mail address, rather than through the dating website, which I did not check often, and he responded, "If I remember." He continued to write through the dating website, though.

By the time Harry suggested we meet, I had lost interest, but my "kiss every frog" attitude prevailed. I suggested a nearby Starbucks, where we could sit, converse, and get to know each other. I clearly described where the coffee shop was located.

He responded, "I don't know where it is. Let's meet at the thrift store at Highway 5 and 92."

"Do you mean Park Avenue Thrift?" I asked.

"I don't know the name," his note said.

How was I to know for sure which store was the right one? I told him to give me his cell number, in case I was late or in the wrong place. He did, but said, "No text messages." Hm. The guy didn't own a phone that would accept a text message? What kind of person believes in abundance but carries a phone so limited that he can't receive a text message? I chose to ignore the hints. (Oh, why?)

On the dot I arrived at the thrift store, but no one was waiting outside, although we had said we would meet outside the store. I went inside and looked around, but saw no one who matched the unsmiling photo he had posted on his profile. After a few minutes I walked back outside and called his cell. He answered and said he was there. Where? I looked left and right. No one who looked like his photo was standing in front of the store.

Instead he stepped out of a car in a handicapped spot in front of the building. His car had a handicap hangtag descending from the rear-view mirror, so he had the legal right to park there, but he strode up to me easily, clearly not physically challenged. I decided not to question him regarding his parking or his health; I had my own issues that I wasn't willing to disclose.

Like his photo, he didn't smile. He simply said, "Let's go inside."

Once in the store, he fingered some of the purses that were the first items we reached. "Not good ones," he said. He stopped for a moment, moved a little closer, and conspiratorially whispered, "The best thrift shops are in Buckhead and Sandy Springs, where you can find Coach, Gucci, and other name-brand handbags worth hundreds of dollars for only five dollars."

Why would he care about women's purses? I said nothing. The stench of his bad breath made me not want to hear more, anyway. I inched away.

Next he pulled out a pair of women's pants on a hanger and shook his head. "You can find Ann Taylor, Ralph Lauren, and stuff like that at those other stores."

First of all, we were in Woodstock, an almost rural area near Atlanta, not Buckhead, a thriving, upscale part of Atlanta. Second, I don't wear designer clothes, but I said nothing.

He finally asked me a question: "Do you ever buy or sell anything on eBay?"

I answered, "I've bought things on eBay, but I've never sold anything there."

He pursed his lips and shook his head as if I should know better. "You can make lots of money selling things on eBay."

"So I've heard, but it depends on how you want to spend your time. That's not how I want to spend mine. Have you ever sold anything on eBay?"

"Not yet, but I'm thinking about it." He looked off in the distance, as if envisioning his future. "I heard of a woman who sold used purses on eBay. She made as much as $20,000 in a year." He continued with several similar stories, ending each one with something such as "He made $25,000."

"It depends on how you want to spend your time," I reiterated.

"Do you like to make money?" Hey! He'd asked a second question, although again, one that could be answered "yes" or "no."

"I do, but . . ." I stopped. I didn't want to repeat myself. I didn't explain that I hate shopping and that I have no interest in spending my time shopping for and selling tangible items. I don't want to store and track inventory, fill orders, pack them up, and take them to the post office. I love my career as an editor, selling my expertise without a great deal of scut work. In addition, why is he impressed with $25,000? How much did it cost for the people to buy and store inventory and post it for sale? How much time did it take the person to locate items, buy them, post them for sale, and fill orders? It could tie up a great deal of money in inventory, be a full-time job, and pay only $20,000 a year. Ugh.

"So you're hoping to find things at thrift shops that you can sell on eBay?" I asked.

"I've already bought lots of things, mostly car parts for older-model cars, but I haven't posted anything for sale yet."

Uh-oh. Do I spot a hoarder? I had already dealt with a prior boyfriend who bought everything from building supplies to office supplies in bulk, stored items from floor to ceiling in his house, and never got rid of or used any of the stuff. Visiting his chaotic, cluttered house used to make me fear I might go insane. The soundtrack from an Alfred Hitchcock murder scene often ran through my mind.

Okay, I've digressed. Harry and I were maybe fifteen feet inside the store by that time, and I was ready to go home. How can a couple carry on a meaningful conversation in a thrift store? How do I make a graceful but quick exit? I increased my pace; we had a lot of store to cover, if I was going to make it through the store and out the door. He scurried up behind me. I tried to walk away, pretending to show interest in something he wasn't interested in and also skipping over an aisle or two, but along he came, still talking about reselling items on eBay. He had asked me only two questions and appeared to care nothing about getting to know me. Instead he kept up a steady banter about eBay, even though I clearly had expressed no interest.

On through the store we went, my feet getting progressively more sore and my mind repeating, "Get me the hell out of here, please, God." Before we reached the door, he had asked me three questions. The third was, "What's the name of your dog?" When he told me the name of his dog, it turned out to be the he-man name he'd used for his profile. Okay, that was cute.

The door was in sight. All I had to do was traverse the final disorderly aisle and freedom would be mine. I tried to rush past the toys, but he stopped me at a large bin of model cars. He sorted through the pile saying, "Collectors'll pay big bucks for some of these."

"But they're just toys, toys manufactured in the hundreds of thousands, probably."

He ignored my protest. "This is a 1970 Camaro Z-twenty-eight. It had a 350 cubic engine." He lifted another. "This is a 1980 Corvette three-oh-five. I'm surprised they turned this model into a Hot Wheels car. The Corvette didn't sell well that year. It came out during bad economic times." He put down the package and grabbed yet another, ignoring my glazed look. "Ah, a 2004 Ford Mustang GT convertible. Cool. This was the fortieth anniversary edition."

"The only thing I care about cars is that they start and run," I said, turning with longing toward the door.

He held up another bubble pack, pointed to some specific feature, and jabbered on. I no longer could hear anything he said. I was in my own world, my feet and my mind screaming for relief.

Oh God, kill me now. The display stand held dozens more cars. I glanced at my watch and stared achingly at the exit, only feet away. Finally I managed to inch forward and reach the door, where I was about to say good-bye when he spotted a consignment shop next door. It actually interested me, too, so when he suggested we go there, I agreed, wishing I could go without him.

Inside I took a quick trek around, between, and among the cluttered and useless merchandise before popping out the door again.

Out front he said, "Let's look over there and see what they have." He pointed to an outdoor flea market in the parking lot.

"I've seen enough," I said, meaning much more than I expressed. I was careful not to say anything encouraging.

"Maybe I'll see you again," he offered.

I may have rolled my eyes, but I said nothing and walked toward my car. He started to walk me there but fell away. Maybe at long last his alleged intuition kicked in.

Why, if he was caring, as his profile claimed, did he not meet me where I first suggested, where we could sit comfortably and have a two-way conversation? Why in heaven's name would he want to meet a woman for the first time at a thrift store? Why would he blather on relentlessly about eBay, cars, and car parts, when I showed no interest? Why would he ask so little about me or my interests? In what world did he think that his behavior could attract a woman?

I've called him Harry because I desperately wanted to "harry up" and get out of there, but now I fear I've bored my readers as much as he bored me.

* * *

Bobbie Christmas, a writer and editor who lives in Georgia, has been single most of her life. She founded Zebra Communications, a book-editing firm, in 1992, and it is still going strong. In her senior years she has enjoyed writing about her odd, awkward, and funny experiences in the dating world.

My Sleep Apnea Test
Linda Parsons

When we reach a "certain age," we may tend to put on a few pounds and snore. I'm seventy-six, so my doctor, concerned about my weight gain, decided that sleep apnea might be a contributing factor. She sent me for an overnight sleep apnea test, which I dreaded.

I arrived around 8:15 PM as instructed. I was shown to a bedroom, where they told me to put on my jammies and sit in a chair. It was freezing, so I asked for a blanket. For the next two hours I watched TV and read. About 10:00 PM my tech, Eddie, came in and hooked me up to all the necessary monitors. He marked spots on my head with grease pencil and then glued wires on. I probably still have mounds of goo in my hair. The ones on bare skin he taped on. He told me that if I needed to go to the bathroom, all I had to do is speak into my nose microphone and he would be right there to unhook me.

My little adventure was even worse than anticipated. I had about twenty wires attached to my head, face, and legs, plus a band around my chest and around my waist, plus tubes and a microphone up my nose! I also had a monitor taped to my index finger, which glowed with a red light. Now...sleep. Are you kidding?

I got in the bed (with my own pillow) and tried to read. I was reading *The Bloodletter's Daughter*, which has a lot about leeches in it. I could at least be thankful that these wires were not drawing blood. I read until about 11:30 PM.

I tried to sleep. The microphone up my nose was driving me crazy, so I dislodged it, but it stuck me in the eye, so I had to put it back. The red light on my finger was like sleeping with Rudolph. As I tried to get comfortable, restricted by all the paraphernalia, I got the giggles. There I was, all alone, lying in bed, laughing like a maniac. The tech could hear my every sound, so I'm sure he thought he had a loony tune in that room. Finally I slept fitfully but woke about 12:30 AM. I was *wide awake.* I rolled over. Or at least I tried. It was a real struggle to roll over and take all that equipment with me, then get my legs untangled and my finger tucked somewhere where the red light didn't shine in my eyes.

Still wide awake. I spoke softly into the microphone in my nose, "Eddie, I can't sleep." Eddie, my keeper, brought me a blessed little sleeping pill, which he said was very mild. I thankfully took the pill, closed my eyes, and conked out. Didn't wake until 5:15 AM. Called Eddie to get unhooked to go to the bathroom. Actually, I had to call four times. I think he was catching a few zzzzzs himself. Finally he came. When I looked at myself in the bathroom mirror, I got the giggles again. Oh, if I'd only had a camera, this would have been the selfie to end all selfies. Wires were taped all over and attached to a main console about

6 x 6 that hung around my neck, and my hair was sticking straight out between the wires.

I had asked Eddie how many hours of sleep he needed for a good test, and he said, "At least four." Well, I had had more than four, so at 5:30 AM I asked if I could go home. They were planning to get me up at 6:00 anyway. He said, "Sure." Amen, amen, and amen.

Home at last, I put my pillow back on my own beautiful bed, turned off the phone, and slept peacefully until 9:00.

Thank goodness it's over. Results showed "borderline sleep apnea." I tried a CPAP machine for about thirty minutes and decided I'd rather be fat and die early.

* * *

Linda J. Parsons grew up in Montana and also has lived in Minnesota and Massachusetts. About twenty-five years ago, she finally got smart and moved to Naples, Florida. She is a retired investment advisor/financial planner. She has two sons and three fabulous grandchildren. She is attempting to write a family history and a family cookbook for her grandchildren. Her hobbies include reading, watercolor painting, writing, and cooking.

Second Marriage...or Not?
Iris E. Price

After being happily divorced for twenty-five years, with both sons educated, holding good jobs, and owning ttheir own homes (in other words, no longer living with Mom—that's me), I decided I might like to get married again. Not soon, but some day. Maybe.

I'd been dating nice men off and on, but eventually we'd lose interest in each other. I had a good job, lots of friends, and my own home. I also had two dogs and several chickens for companionship.

So why, at age fifty-six, did I decide I wanted to try marriage again?

I'm still trying to answer that question.

I worked at a government job in downtown San Diego during the day and taught a fitness class at the YMCA several evenings after work. I drove my car to downtown San Diego, parked on a bridge near the building where I worked (so I didn't have to pay for parking), and walked the rest of the way to the office.

One day I got back to my car and found the windows broken. My beautiful old VW had been smashed and robbed! Those were the days before everyone had a smartphone or even any kind of cell phone, but someone came by and saw the broken windows and asked if he could help me. He found a phone and called the police. The police took a report, and someone else came by who had a newspaper with him. He offered me the newspaper to sit on while I drove my car to the repair shop so I wasn't sitting in broken glass.

I had the car repaired but followed the police officer's advice not to park on the bridge anymore, as cars were always being broken into there. I got a bus pass and started parking my car near the bus stop so I could have it there to drive to the YMCA, and started taking the bus to work. I worked for the city of San Diego, and employees were able to get a discounted rate on bus passes.

The same group of people, many of whom were city employees, rode the bus to work every weekday morning. The bus arrived at 6:20 AM, so people started arriving at about 6:00 to be sure not to miss the bus. People talked together while waiting for the bus, and soon I felt like I was part of the group.

There were a couple of people who stood away from the group and read. One was a bald man, maybe my age, who never spoke to anyone. He sat at the back of the bus; I sat toward the front. When we saw each other we exchanged "good morning"s, and that was it.

One day I didn't have to teach at the Y after work, so I left my car at home, walked to the bus stop, and then walked home. On the way home, I happened to look across the street, and there was the bald guy walking in the same direction as I was, but on the other side of the main street. At the same corner as each other, he turned left and I turned right.

I'd been running for many years, and most days I'd run on my lunch break. On weekends I'd do an early morning run—*really* early—in my neighborhood. The police advised those of us who were out early to run in the street, as running on the sidewalk left us vulnerable to being attacked by people hiding behind parked cars or near buildings.

I was about a mile from home and running down a hill when I heard footsteps running behind me; I also heard my heart thump in fear. I immediately took my pepper spray canister out of my pocket, twisted the sprayer to the "on" position, and kept it hidden in the palm of my hand, ready to use, just like the police had trained me to do. I'm a slow runner, and it didn't take long before the footsteps were right behind me. I quickly turned around, pepper spray ready, and was surprised to see the bald guy from the bus running behind me. He recognized me and slowed down to my pace.

I didn't spray him!

We discovered that we both worked for the city but in different buildings. We knew many of the same people but, until the bus stop, our paths had never crossed. He said he and his wife were discussing divorce (likely story), and he would like to date me. Oh, and he said his name was Grant.

"No, thanks. You're still married."

Fast-forward about six months. We both still took the 6:20 bus to work. Eventually he told me that he had filed for divorce but still lived in the same house with his wife. I met him at work events at lunch, such as special programs, and occasionally went for runs with him on our lunch break.

One day he knocked on my door. He said a co-worker who knows us both had told him where I lived. He was polite and clean and said the divorce was proceeding. I let him in. My dogs liked him. The chickens weren't interested until he tossed them some grain.

These casual get-togethers continued. I asked when his divorce would be final, and he said he was "legally separated."

I let him meet my older son, a paramedic, who has very good judgment about people. Sometimes I should listen to him.

My son and I went to eat at an all-you-can-eat soup-and-salad bar, and Grant met us there. My son told me to get my food and "Take your time." Oh-oh.

He grilled Grant about everything, including why he was still living with his wife if he was legally separated, and when was he getting this divorce he'd been talking about. Later, my son called me and said one word: "NO!"

I didn't listen.

About six months later, Grant moved into my house with me. He said he'd left his house to his wife, including most of the furniture. He asked if I'd marry him when his divorce was final. I asked when his divorce would be final. He then told me that he was still legally separated and hadn't filed for divorce. I told him to take his few belongings and move out of my house, to which he answered that he'd file for divorce.

"When?"

"Right away."

"*When?*"

"Okay, right now."

And he did.

I believed him when I saw the legal paperwork. It was then that I discovered that he was three years younger than I. Oh, well, as the saying goes, "Get them young and bring them up right!" Right?

By now my close friends and co-workers knew of the relationship and got to know Grant. It wasn't a positive reaction on the part of my friends. Did I listen? No. When his divorce was final, we got engaged...or anyway, we decided to get married. We also decided to buy a house that we'd both own.

On August 21, 1997, we closed on a run-down 2 1/3-acre property in a rural area of San Diego county. He was out backpacking with friends, so I made sure the deed read with my name first, and "with rights of survivorship," which meant whoever lived longer got the house.

Two days later, on August 23rd, at ages fifty-five (he) and fifty-eight (I), we got married in a park with our closest friends and some relatives in attendance. My sons walked me down the "aisle." However, before we started walking, my older son said he and his brother needed to talk to me. My younger son asked if I knew what I was doing. He added that he and his wife, who was at the wedding, had a spare bedroom and wanted me to come live with them. They live in Alabama. It was a nice offer, but I politely refused. I don't like Alabama although I love my son and his wife.

Then my older son said, "Mom, rather than walk down the aisle, why don't we take a vacation in Mexico? We can be there in less than an hour." Funny kid.

"No, I'm going through with this."

Then my older son said, "Mom, we'd like you to keep our last name instead of changing it to his."

I was noncommittal.

Then, with one son on each side of me, we walked down the aisle. All of a sudden I noticed that my matron of honor, a ninety-two-year-old woman with whom I'd been friends for many years, wasn't there. We stopped in our tracks, and my older son called Helen, my friend. She said she'd thought the wedding was next week.

Sure she did.

So another friend, this one in her eighties, said she'd be matron of honor, but she'd have to sit down to do it.

Fine. Let's proceed.

A friend of my fiancé officiated at the ceremony. He made it brief and then pronounced us "man and wife," even though I'd made him promise to pronounce us "wife and husband." Too late. I'd chew him out later.

My new husband said to me, "Now that you're my property..." and my decision was made. I didn't take his last name but kept the same one as my sons have.

We had a small reception at my house (yes, it was still only mine), and one of his backpacking friends ate all the hors d'oeuvres before anyone else could get them. Oink!

We didn't take a honeymoon since we'd planned to work on the new house on weekends. Back at the office on Monday, one of my co-workers said

"I hear you bought the farm."

"No, John," I replied, "I bought *a* farm." He laughed. I wonder if that was a deliberate mistake.

It took us a year of weekends to get the farm livable. We drove up there in two vehicles every Saturday, each of us taking one of our dogs, and drove back to San Diego every Sunday night so we could get ready to go to work the next day.

Our farm is now home to us, two rescue dogs, three rescue goats, four hens, and two roosters, one of which crows the first four notes of Beethoven's Fifth Symphony.

Despite the advice of all my friends and relatives not to marry this man, I did it. Did it last? We're still working on it. We'll celebrate our twenty-second anniversary in August, at which time he'll be seventy-seven and I'll be eighty.

Oh, and remember that old saying I quoted previously about getting them young and bringing them up right? I'll be noncommittal on this one, but sometimes we have to take our chances.

* * *

Iris Price is a Boston native who, as soon as she reached legal age, which was twenty-one in those days, "escaped" from her parents' house, moved to Florida, and eventually to California. At age seventy-eight years and nine months, she finished her PhD in natural medicine. Despite having almost lifelong Crohn's disease and most of her intestines removed at age thirty-six, she's a long-time runner, and is also a Renaissance-Baroque musician who has performed all up and down the West Coast, as far north as Victoria, British Columbia.

Ghost Train
John Sheffield

This is the true story of an experience my stepfather-in-law had. It wasn't funny to him at the time, but it may be funny to you now....

At breakfast one morning in the 1970s, my wife's stepfather, Victor, announced he needed to get some money from his bank in London and would take the ten o'clock train into Paddington Station. He had made this trip many times. Back then, the trains were punctual, so he was ready to board when, at about ten, the train arrived.

His compartment had facing bench seats, with three women and two men facing each other. Victor had a quick look at the women. None caught his fancy, so he immediately started to read the book he'd brought with him. Absorbed in his book, he paid little attention to the other passengers, noting only that another couple got on during a brief stop at Reading Station. The clickety-click of the wheels on the rails had a soporific effect, and he began to drop off. Clickety-click, clickety-click...click, click, click...he looked up. The train was switching tracks to the left; maybe the platform would be a different one than before. He looked at his watch: 10:55—odd. Normally the ride took around fifty minutes; they should have reached Paddington by now. Then the train entered a tunnel, and Victor did not remember a tunnel. They remained in darkness for a few minutes. Victor was getting worried.

When they emerged into the light, Victor looked at his fellow passengers. They appeared unconcerned, but Victor was worried.

"This may sound like a silly question," he said, "but where is this train going?"

They all laughed.

"It is a silly question," a woman said, giggling.

"Why?"

"Because we don't know."

The passengers were now giving Victor their full attention.

"I'm sorry. I don't understand what you mean." Victor was really worried now.

"You're joking," somebody muttered.

"No. Where are we going?"

"We don't know. This is a mystery tour."

Can you imagine the shock? Victor had never heard of such a thing.

"A what?" Victor asked.

"We all paid to take a day trip on this train," a florid-faced man answered. "The fun part is that we don't know where it will take us, except it will be on the coast somewhere."

"I thought we were going to the south coast," a lady in a floral dress said. "But we're going north of London, so I guess it will be the east coast."

"Probably Southend or Ipswich," the man suggested.

Victor was horrified. "They're miles away, and I have to get to my bank before it closes at three. When will we get there?"

"Between twelve-thirty and one, we were told."

"But then I'd have to get a train back. I'll never make it to the bank in time."

"Looks like it," the lady replied sympathetically.

When Victor got home that night, he told me this story. I remember asking him what was going through his mind when the lady said they didn't know where they were going.

"I thought I had died," Victor replied. "I knew the old ticker had given out at last, Jane. I was on the train that takes you to the Pearly Gates and Saint Peter. Or worse, I was in a Fellini film."

"What did you do?" I said.

"Well, shortly after the revelation about the tour, the train stopped at a signal," Victor replied. "I opened the door and got out by the side of the track. The passengers shouted encouragement as I scrambled up the embankment. I soon found out the place was a park in the Golders Green area of north London, a few miles from the city. Nearby was a tube station." Victor grinned. "I made it to the bank in time. Not bad for a septuagenarian."

* * *

John Sheffield retired in 2003 from the Oak Ridge National Laboratory, where he was the director for energy technology programs. Subsequently, he was a senior fellow at the Institute for a Secure and Sustainable Environment (ISSE) at the University of Tennessee, Knoxville. His particular interests are:
- The opportunities for fusion energy, including options to enhance its attractiveness.
- World population growth and future energy demand and resources.
- The connection of energy use to the environment.
- Writing, as a member of the Atlanta Writers Club.

He has been writing for many decades, including contributions to a compilation of short stories by local authors, *North Point of View: Tales of Alpharetta and Beyond.* Among his other recent publications are: the chapter on "Future World Energy Needs and Resources," in *Energy, the Environment, and the Pursuit of Sustainability*; *Plasma Scattering of Electromagnetic Radiation;* and a humorous memoir, *Fun in Fusion Research*—the subject of talks at DragonCon in 2013 and 2014 and two mysteries, *Roseland's Secret* and *Return to Roseland.* He coordinated and contributed to the anthology, *The Treasure Trove: A Collection of Prose and Poetry.* He won the Southeastern Writers Association's Edna Sampson Award for the novel *My Friend Albert.*

Hurrah for Subtitles
Beverly Lessard

I never thought I'd see the day when my first question when watching a movie would be, "Does it have subtitles?"

Even with my two high tech supersonic hearing aids, I often have trouble understanding what the actors are saying, especially when they whisper. I know it can be important to the plot, but I don't think directors should allow their actors to whisper at any time, ever. This only causes the boomer-aged audience to wear out their remotes as they adjust the volume control up and down. Or worse, they ask someone in the room what was just said, the latter resulting in both of them missing the next three lines. This is not only frustrating for everyone involved but can often be the first reason listed in divorce cases.

And I have to laugh when I think of all the years my husband wrestled with the remote to get subtitles to go away. Sometimes he'd have to restart the movie three or four times. Now I seek them out as if they hold the secret to the meaning of life. Because seriously, they just might.

Even with reruns, shows I've seen over and over again, I can't always remember if Barney Fife told Andy Griffith to jump in the lake or that he just bumped the cake. I certainly don't want to be misquoting any of those old shows and be responsible for changing how history views the '50s.

Some movies I've seen so many times, I can almost mouth all the lines—movies like *It's a Wonderful Life*, *Casablanca* and *Harvey*. Remember all the great old BC movies? "BC"—Before Color.

I remember years ago trying to get our teenage daughters to watch one of the old classics. Without hesitation, they informed me that they couldn't possibly watch anything in black and white. Those movies were way too primitive, as in: gag me with a spoon! Even to suggest it was a character flaw on my part. I assured them that they were missing some of the best movies ever made, movies starring Shirley Temple, Humphrey Bogart, and Clark Gable. And they assured me that they didn't care.

At least I was smart enough not to suggest any of Charlie Chaplin's flicks, which were not only in black and white but also had no sound, just a moving picture, usually at the wrong speed, with a few lines typed at the bottom. They would have considered watching those nothing short of extra homework. And they would have been partially correct.

Subtitles actually provide an educational component to movie watching. Just as my typing skills have improved with the invention of email, my reading skills have accelerated to the speed-reading level. I find it challenging to finish the sentence before the next one appears. Sometimes I finish reading the subtitles so quickly, I have time to glance at the picture.

Yes, thanks to subtitles, life is good once again! I can follow the plot and not disrupt my husband's viewing pleasure. Of course, don't ask me if the glass of water in the last scene suddenly filled up again at the end. I'm doing well if I know what the actors look like.

* * *

Beverly Lessard is the author of several humorous books including *Relentlessly Upbeat* and *Knee Deep in Sawdust and Fudge Brownie Mix,* and one serious one: *Are You Emotionally Ready to Retire?* A New England resident, she is a mother and proud grandma, loves to write, and particularly enjoys golf.

A Few Quickies from the ALF
Lenna Buissink

I volunteer in an assisted living facility, and some residents were happy to share snippets of stories. None of these is long enough for a chapter by itself, but I hope you and your readers get a kick out of these briefs from the residents of the ALF.

. . .

I was talking to one of the ALF residents, LeAnn, who is ninety-two, and I confessed to her a recent embarrassing incident that had happened to me.

I am sixty-seven. I was in a parking lot, and I had a UTI and a bad cough. As I unlocked my car and coughed, I wet my pants. (I'm glad I was finished shopping.) As I told this story to LeAnn, she started laughing and laughing. I said "LeAnn, this is not funny. *I wet my pants!*" She threw back her head and laughed even harder. I asked her, "LeAnn, why are you laughing?"

Between peals of laughter, she managed to gasp out, "Because it wasn't me!"

. . .

This happened to Louise before she moved into the ALF. She was in Wal-Mart and walked out talking to a neighbor. She could *not* find her car. She looked and looked and looked and finally called her granddaughter to tell her she couldn't find her car and it might have been stolen. The granddaughter started laughing.

Louise demanded, "What's so funny about my car being lost?"

The granddaughter answered, "Grandma, I just helped Grandpa find his car at the hardware store."

• • •

My grandmother had a pill box where she put her daily pills. It worked just fine until she got a new pill that was too big to fit in the box with the others. She kept her new pill bottle next to her pill box so she would remember to take the new pill. Sadly, she still forgot to take it. But then she came up with an idea: "I know! I'll put a button in the pill box, and when I see the button, it will remind me to take the new big pill."

The next day she went to take her pill and looked for the button. You guessed it. She had swallowed the button along with the other pills.

• • •

Madeline and her neighbor had gone to a mall and spent the day shopping. When they came out, they couldn't find the car. They looked for an hour and a half, and in every section of the parking lot. Finally they sat down back inside the mall and tried to remember where they had parked.

That's when they remembered they had brought the white car, not the red one.

• • •

Leonard couldn't find his glasses. He was in a hurry for an appointment, so instead of spending any more time looking for them, he bought a pair of readers at a convenience store on his way. When they asked him to fill out some paperwork at the appointment, he reached in his pocket for his new glasses, but the receptionist said, "Why don't you use the ones perched on your head?"

...

Harriet had been rear-ended the week before her scheduled trip with her friends to go gambling at a nearby casino. The insurance company had loaned her a car. The ladies enjoyed a good day, gambling, dining, and just having fun. When they left the casino, they remembered parking in a handicapped parking spot but couldn't find their car. The security police came out and looked with them to no avail. It was suggested they go in and fill out a stolen car report.

When asked for the license plate number, it dawned on them that they were not driving Harriet's own car.

* * *

Lenna Buissink is a sixty-seven-year-old retired school teacher. She volunteers in an assisted living facility in Walla Walla, Washington.

Crooked Toes
Deborah Robinson

"Dave, come here quick! Look at my big toes and tell me what you think! They're crooked, and it must've just happened! I'm sure they were straight when we arrived here just two months ago! Doesn't it seem that it would happen more gradually than that? Oh man, I'd better get them checked when we get home to Michigan. What if it's arthritis? Do you think I should find a doctor in Florida? They may see a lot of that."

My sweetheart looked at my worrisome toes, bent over, gently touched one, and asked if it hurt. "Um, no but just look—the right one is the worst! What makes things get crooked like that? Crooked legs, backs, necks, and some of those fingers I've seen! I guess it must be about aging, huh? I just didn't think it would happen yet! I'd better get used to it. Let me see your toes. Oh my—you've got it too! Oh honey!"

Dave had the iPad in his hand and was reading what Google had to say about crooked toes. "Deb, according to the Mayo Clinic site this is a natural part of aging. The toes, fingers, and all of our bones can change their positions. As long as it doesn't hurt, isn't inflamed or causing a problem in your gait, the treatment is to do nothing. It'll be okay, honey; we're just getting a bit older."

Leave it to Dave to have a logical answer for this new crooked toe phenomenon. He doesn't even appear rattled as he takes another quick inventory of his own toes, puts on his socks, and looks my way. "Deb, you do realize that we've both passed our sixtieth birthdays, right? Technically, we're past being middle aged unless we're going to live to be 120 and 124 years old!

"Statistics say that the average life expectancy of men in the United States is 75.6—but honey, I have some good news for you!! You are expected to live to be 80.8 years old. Of course, if you were living in Niger you'd likely be dying as we speak and I'd have checked out 2.2 years ago! How lucky are we! Those other folks probably don't have time to get crooked toes or anything else for that matter!"

This man never disappoints me with his heartfelt facts! Shaking my head and dragging my aging self to the couch, I flop down. I perch my feet on the footstool and take one last look at my crossed ankles as my darling speaks up one more time. "I just read that varicose veins can be avoided by keeping your feet elevated, wearing compression socks, and exercising. Crossing your legs is a no-no. There'll be no more sitting like that, Missy!

"Deb, I'm so glad we found this website. I'm saving it to your Favorites! We can use it for all kinds of references. Here's something you need to know about those naps you've been taking in your chair. That's going to have to stop, too! It says here that it causes bad posture and isn't good for your spine! Listen to this, will you? 'Slouching in your chair or as you walk can impair digestion, cause constipation, and even affect healthy breathing.'

"Just one last thing, Deb—you know your glass of wine in the afternoon? Well, it should not exceed 5 ounces. I'm pretty sure you aren't following that! I am getting out a measuring cup and marking the 5-ounce line with a red Sharpie. That should completely take the guesswork out of Happy Hour!"

Nap time and Happy Hour are my favorites! "Sweetheart, put that iPad down and pour me a glass of wine, please. Now, put that measuring cup away. I've decided that my toes aren't going to be a big problem in my life. Some new beaded sandals should distract from my crooked appendages. Save that wine for later because I'm going out for a bit. I'll be back in a little while. Bealls has a sale on shoes and I need to stop by Beach Liquor Store. A six-bottle wine purchase takes a full ten percent off the total price! Pretty awesome, I'd say! Could you please take a couple of steaks out of the freezer? I could go for a nice grilled one for dinner tonight."

My sweetheart studies the computer intently and then chirps up, "I'm not so sure that's a good idea, honey. Listen to this: 'Following a vegan diet can add considerable years to your life!' Want to try some grilled tofu for dinner tonight? Recipes.com has oodles of healthy ways to prepare tofu. I just saw some at Publix the other day! Could you pick some of these ingredients up while you're out? Honey did you hear me?"

  I wonder how long he'll keep talking before he notices I've left? I'd better get to Beach Liquors before they close!

* * *

Deborah ("Debbie") Robinson has been wintering in Rotonda West, Florida for ten years. She retired rather young from a Michigan school system. She has watched herself, her sweetheart, and thousands of other seniors travel down this aging path. Sometimes she's found herself laughing and crying from what she's learned by observation. Yes, she admits, sometimes the crying happens when she looks in the mirror.

  Publishing short stories, belonging to writing groups, naps, and cocktail parties take up a lot of her hours. Hanging with her awesome grandchildren takes time and lots of energy, but she finds their youthful attitudes are contagious. She truly recommends retirement to all who are eligible! However, she cautions, don't take life too seriously, and don't forget to laugh!

Getting It Done in Florida
Margaret Jane Jones

We have a snug little house
With a thirty-year roof
Where we can hide out and lie low.
We have patchy grass in front and back,
And cabbage palms and live oaks guarding
every side.

We have a Walmart up the road,
Grocery stores galore,
And a Big Boys' Barbecue nearby
Where we can satisfy that once-a-month urge
To step out on the town, splurge, and chow
down.

We have a bit of income trickling in,
And an ought-one Honda that runs.
We have the Internet and Twitter
If we want to fritter, and then there's the
beach
Where we can sit, sun, and swim.

We have no early wake-up calls,
No deadlines, no schedules at all.
What we have most of is time—
Time to ponder, time to putter, and
Time to grow old—
And we can tell you, my friend, we're getting
it done.

* * *

Margaret Jane Jones began writing late in life and has written and illustrated *The Sun-Up Series:* four books for children ages eight to twelve, a picture book: *Wild Perfumes from a Winter Wood* for young readers, and poetry—much of it pertaining to dwindling wilderness lands in the state of New Hampshire. For detailed information see her website: margaretjanejones.com

Downsizing
Lorraine Harrison

It's inevitable. Avoid it and your stuff will be put on display to be picked over during an estate sale. When there was less stuff to be had, saving things for posterity was all the rage. These days, posterity doesn't want it.

We moved into our house eight years ago. The number of items that remain exactly where we put them in order to get rid of the boxes is astounding. The closets in our two guest bedrooms are full. Visitors can spend the night, but they can't hang anything up. Pictures that were protectively wrapped for the move have yet to be unwrapped. Great-Great-Uncle Somebody looks quite serious in his hat. I tell myself I ought to write people's names on the backs of the pictures in the shoebox in the top of the closet. I'll do it as soon as I get the time. Ever heard of anyone getting time?

The kids are on to us. They refused to take china from my three aunts. They don't want Grandma's silver. It tarnishes. There's no app for that. When our daughter agreed to take a crystal bowl, I was so surprised that I almost dropped it. It was Christmas. That may have softened her resolve.

Some of our stuff came from relatives who were getting rid of their stuff. What a sucker I've been! Who knew? One son wants to keep everything. I've seen his room. He's the hoarder in the family. We offer him things sparingly.

tWe have kitchen gadgets, presents mostly, that slice and dice and do amazing things to vegetables, which we do not use. Occasionally we pull them out, give them a try, and inevitably return them to a dark corner of a cabinet that's hard to reach. We don't need another spatula, no matter how cute or fancy it may be. Recently, I've noticed only two of my four Lord of the Rings goblets on the shelf. Someone must have helped themselves. Isn't that just dandy?

One of my cousins can tell you the name of every relative who originally owned each piece of his furniture in his house. It's like walking through a museum. He still asks me if I want my grandmother's chair, and I still say "No."

Looking around, there are still things I can't part with: the model sailboat my uncle made, a pewter Cossack who looks like he's dancing, the obsidian statue that looks part Easter Island and part Hawaiian Island. Add to that the two stuffed "extra" closets, the china no one will take, and that bunch of kitchen gadgets.

Estate sale, anyone?

* * *

Like many before them, Lorraine and her husband retired and moved to the Sunshine State. They bought a boat ('The Cliché') and fish in the Gulf. Her husband, "MacGyver," is a retired chemist. Now he's the neighborhood's unconventional Mr. Fix-it.

Lorraine's career was in marketing. Now she's a part-time writer. Her first novel, *Grip of Change*, is available on Amazon. A collection of short stories and a second novel are in the works.

Passing Myself on the Stairs: ADD Got the Better of Me
Sharon Love Cook

It was a trendy new cafe: chrome counters, hanging lamps, and jazz playing in the background. The sandwich menu was an old-school blackboard scribbled in chalk. After perusing the list of offerings, I told the bandanna-wearing server I'd have prosciutto and cheese.

"What do you want it on?" he asked.

"Bread."

His smile was patient. "We have ciabatta, croissant, brioche, whole-grain artisanal...." He waited, tapping his pencil on the counter.

"Whole grain."

"How about toppings?" He pointed to another list on the busy blackboard. "You can choose three."

I slipped on my glasses and leaned forward to read. "I'll have lettuce, tomato, sprouts." He nodded at that. "What kind of sprout — mung bean, lentil, alfalfa?" "Alfalfa." I blotted my forehead. I'd made it this far. There was no turning back.

"What about cheese?" He rattled off names. When he got to Gorgonzola, I interrupted. "Do you have American?" At that point I craved the familiarity of the bland, processed squares.

My response must have been loud because the server looked startled. "Sure." He wrote on his pad and, without looking up, said, "Take a seat. We'll call when your order's ready. What's your phone number?"

I told him. Then I added, "It's a landline, and I'll be at home when you call." With that I turned and raced for the door.

As a senior adult with ADD (Attention Deficit Disorder), I'm constantly confronted with an overwhelming barrage of choices. Even the pet food manufacturers have gotten into the act. Our dog's brand now contains gluten-free beet pulp, flaxseed, and added probiotics. Not to be outdone, our cat's food is geared to feline ailments such as urinary tract infection, dental plaque, and hair balls.

When I was a kid, pet food was made by one company: Calo. The product smelled as unappetizing as it looked, but at least purchasing it was easy. It was sold in two varieties: one for cats and one for dogs.

Likewise, the greeting card industry is exploding. Where cards once occupied a rack or two, they now take up three aisles at the supermarket. And, like the pet food manufacturers, they've gotten into sub-categories. I recently hoped to find a simple condolence card. No easy task, I discovered, searching among cards that specified the recipient's relationship to the deceased, e.g. "Sorry for the loss of your mother-in-law." I saw cards intended for great-aunts, step-grandmothers, second cousins. When the industry has run the gamut of family relations, will they expand to the professionals in our lives: "Sorry for the loss of your plumber/lawyer/hairdresser"? When and if that happens, three aisles won't be enough.

ADD runs in families; my mother kept her go-to-church girdle inside a seldom-used electric skillet. For those with this malady, shopping can be perilous. Try going into Starbucks without a plan, or a movie theater with its dozen screens. They don't call it a "complex" for nothing. Surrounded by so much stimuli, I lose track of where I'm heading or where I've been. I call it "passing myself on the stairs."

For instance, the last time I went to the mall, I got so overwhelmed I rushed for the exit. In my haste, I bounced off a free-standing plexiglass panel. The clerks, ignoring me earlier, now helped me off the floor. Needless to say, I avoid malls. My idea of a perfect store contains two racks: "Reduced for Clearance" and "Everything Must Go."

In my opinion, online shopping was designed for ADDers. We can relax and mull over our choices. Nobody is pressuring us, or as my mother used to say of pushy salespeople, "breathing down our necks." To a kid, her words conjured up a world of strange adult behavior.

Maybe someday we'll have service dogs for ADD. Wearing sensors, they'll be alerted when their subjects reach stimulation overload. I could have used such a dog at the trendy cafe. Sensing a meltdown, the specially trained canine would lead me to the exit. There, at the door, he'd pause and lift his leg.

* * *

Sharon Love Cook of Beverly, MA, writes humor columns for *The Salem News* and is the author of *The Granite Cove Mysteries: Come for the Chowder, Stay for the Murder.* She is a cartoonist and has currently published the illustrated gift book: *15 Reasons Why: Men Are for Now, Cats Are Forever.*

Cellphonin' It In
Mark Daponte

There was a time when hearing a parent bark, "Can you please get off the phone so I can use it?" meant his or her child was talking—actually talking!—on the phone and hogging up the lone landline. In these times, imploring a grandson to put down a phone is like trying to take a bone away from a hungry pit bull whose only trick is rolling his eyes in the presence of "know-nothing-and-not-hip" adults. Yes, grandkids spend more time in the wintertime looking at glass than a goldfish in a fishbowl, and both share the same wide-eyed, glazed stare.

Of course, when a grandson is asked to give his phone a rest for a minute, the child will retort something like, "It's not a phone in a phone's sense. It's a pocket TV; which I bet you'd watch constantly too if you were my age. You once said your TV was like a babysitter to you, didn't you?"

And the grandparent will admit that this is true and offer a remark like, "My grandpa used to say, 'Son, when I was your age, I had to 'only' walk *nine* miles to school.' Now, I have to confess my hardship to you. Son, when I was your age, my TV only had *nine* channels…and they weren't on twenty-four hours a day. They all showed test patterns at four a.m.!"

"Huh…what's a test pattern? Is that like reserve rabbit ears in case the rabbit ears antenna breaks?"

There's no point arguing with a person with such a deep well of life experience as an eleven-year-old possesses. So, in an effort to get him to put down the phone, you ask if you can watch one of his favorite videos with him. You shake your head in amazement as you watch rappers and "Instantgram" celebrities (who are relevant for an instant) routinely drop F-bombs and $100 bills in front of their paid stripper friends. Knowing your grandson isn't hip to visual Pablum of the past, you find a common ground and offer a compromise:

"We both love *Batman*, right? How about we see *real* old school *Batman*? Let's stream this guy named Adam West instead of that guy named Kanye West."

You and your DNA match gleefully watch Adam and his sidekick drop villains instead of F-bombs and find that the goofy show still holds up.

And to your shock, you find that your grandson *finally* isn't holding up his cellphone.

* * *

Mark Daponte is an HR consultant for a college in New York City and has sold three short stories, three full-length screenplays, and nine short screenplays, and punches up screenplays—because they don't punch back. He also pens short stories as (alas!) a low-paying side job—though he wishes he could do this full time and work as an HR consultant as a side job.

We'd Better Not Get Married
Cynthia MacGregor

At seventy-five, rounding the corner to seventy-six, I'm what used to be called "living in sin." I love the man I live with, and I'm sure he loves me even though he's not the romantic type and doesn't smother me with kisses. But I don't see any reason to tie the legal knot. We're certainly not in danger of having children "out of wedlock"!

My S.O. and I have a good relationship that's lasted almost twelve years as of this writing. He doesn't bring me flowers, I don't care for most candy (I'm more into spicy foods than sweets, but he doesn't bring me salamis either), he forgets my birthday...but I shrug it off. He earned major brownie points chauffeuring me in a wheelchair during *l'affaire du* broken ankle (you're not one of those people who skips reading the introduction of a book, are you?!), and again when I developed sciatica and we had to haul the wheelchair out of storage.

I consider that I was doing him a favor: He doesn't get much exercise, but pushing that wheelchair around our condo must surely have strengthened his arms and legs. Hmm...maybe I should have sent him a bill for physical therapy!

He does have his flaws. The older he gets, the more persnickety he gets about food. Since we're too broke to eat out more than once in a rare blue moon, and the moon has been yellow every time I've looked at it lately, that means I'm cooking again tonight.

And every night. But so many of the foods that pleased his twelve-years-ago palate no longer appeal to his taste.

But he does the dishes almost every night. Except...he leaves grease and food particles on many of the dishes he washes. I consider it an obvious bid to have me "fire him" as family dishwasher and take the job back myself, but I'm not falling for that. I put the yucchhy dishes back in the sink for re-washing. And don't tell me his "senior" eyes missed seeing the grease and particles. Eyes may lose their acuity with age, but there's nothing wrong with the tactile ability of his hands to *feel* what's wrong with the dishes.

And speaking of washing the dishes, this man is so intent on saving money that he uses paper plates and then washes them for re-use!

Although I'm still working (self-employed), Grant is totally dependent on Social Security, and he doesn't get much. Our financial deal is that I pay the utilities, the insurance, the condo maintenance, and the mortgage (the condo having been mine before I ever met Grant, it's in my name), and he pays for our food and the one luxury he gives in to: a three-hours-a-week housecleaner. So, like many other seniors, we do a once-a-month major shopping trip on his "payday." We usually run out of many food items between paydays, but he's often out of money with which to get replacements. Seniorhood is a b*tch.

Talk about being out of money—my car has been without air-conditioning for two years now because I don't have the almost-$800 needed to fix it—and we live in South Florida, land of the perennial summer. The car is nearly twenty years old but runs great, although it's badly in need of a paint job.

Fortunately for my budget I have never gone in for "retail therapy." My idea of therapy is a couple of glasses of scotch—and if I had to go shopping, I would definitely need that scotch afterward. To me, shopping is a torture. It's a good thing I never changed careers and went in for spy craft. Merely suggesting I *might* be forced to go shopping would be enough to make me give up every state secret I possessed.

There are definite advantages to relationships as a senior. For one thing, in the holiday season, there's no arguing about whose side of the family we're going to have Thanksgiving dinner and Christmas dinner with. Our respective parents are long since dead, as is my daughter; he's estranged from his sons; I'm estranged from my grandsons; and my darling granddaughter is grown but not yet married and busy living her own life many states north of us. We stay home and invite friends.

Another holiday advantage: Money is tight, but at this stage of our lives, there's darned little either of us wants, so we don't exchange presents. Not only does that excuse me from the dreaded shopping trip (although I thank and bless Amazon for those times when I do have to buy something), but it absolves us both from pretending something wrong-o or even hideous was "just what I wanted" and then figuring out how to surreptitiously return or exchange it.

Another advantage to senior relationships: Seniors are more apt to snore. Now, you may think that's a *dis*advantage, but I simply love it when I wake up in the middle of the night and hear him snoring. Really! No sarcasm intended. First of all, it reminds me that he's there, in my bed and in my life, and second, it tells me he's asleep and not having a bad night of wakefulness. To me, it's a very comforting sound.

My S.O. loves to live naked. When we first started living together, his propensity for nudity didn't evince itself. It started to rear its head at the same time he put on a lot of weight, and I don't think that was a coincidence. His shorts (remember, this is Florida—year-round shorts weather) wouldn't close properly, and even the ones that might fit a trained elephant were tight on him. So he took to living naked.

To tell the truth, I enjoy the free feeling of divesting myself of my clothes too, but I won't run around the apartment nude when the blinds are open, as he does. I wait till at least three o'clock if not later, then close the blinds, and only then do I strip.

Maybe we should move to a nudist colony—or maybe I should post a sign outside our windows: NUDE MAN VIEWING and charge people to look in the windows.

Nah. In his seventies and...um...portly, he looks more like a beached whale than the star of a porno flick. Viewers are likely to ask for double their money back!

I've had a full set of dentures since I was in my early forties. I had bad teeth, and I thought that the major work the dentist proposed to do was a bad investment. "Pull 'em all and give me fake ones," I directed. I've never regretted it—except for the time I coughed and the teeth flew out of my mouth—in public.

Grant, on the other hand, has all his own teeth. Let's just not talk about what condition they're in. He avoids the dentist like I avoid shopping!

As I said earlier, we've been living together almost twelve years as of this writing, but neither of us feels the need to "make it legal." And if the wedding was preceded by a shower, what would we do with all that stuff we'd receive as shower gifts and then wedding presents? It's not like we're first setting up housekeeping. We have everything we need...and lots of stuff we don't. (Why have so many people gifted us with perfumed candles? Is it a hint our home is malodorous? Or one of us is?) If we got married and got un-needed shower gifts and wedding gifts, in this small condo apartment, where would we store it all? We might have to buy a second condo apartment just to keep the stuff in. Oh—that's right—no money.

Well then, we'd better not get married.

* * *

Cynthia MacGregor not only conceived and edited this book, she has over 100 more published books to her credit, most of them books she actually wrote herself as opposed to soliciting suitable material. (For specifics, you are invited to visit www.cynthiamacgregor.com). She is addicted to her work as a freelance writer/editor and works seven days a week, starting at some insane hour. (She typically gets up around four or five and, after a quick stop in the bathroom and a detour to the kitchen to get a glass of iced coffee, she's in her in-home office, catching up on the email that came in after five the night before, when she abandoned her beloved computer to spend time with her even more beloved S.O.) Her friends call her "The Energizer Bunny" because she never stops going, and she happily proclaims that "There's no one in the world I'd want to trade lives with." She has hosted two different podcast series, two different TV series in her South Florida area (all these were interview shows), and had around a dozen of her one-act plays produced, mostly by a now-defunct community theatre in her area, although one, a show for family audiences, had a respectable run in New York. As of this writing she is producing an animated Christmas TV special she hopes to sell to a network for airing in the 2019 Christmas season. It's adapted from her book *Heartfelt, the Special Reindeer,* a follow-on to which, *The Boy Who Didn't Believe in Santa,* will be published for the 2019 Christmas season.

86

Old is a Word
By Bob Lebensold

Old is a word.
Seventy-eight is a number.
Your call.

Most men my age are dragging their asses more than I drag mine.

I eat what I want, take one prostate pill a day, and about five days a week have a hefty double shot of Jameson's on the rocks. It mellows me out.

I have not lost interest in the many lovely ladies who grace this Florida snowbird destination

I go to yoga at eight every morning, to the pavilion on the beach for the music most nights, and take my turn as the entertainer on Tuesdays: an hour and a half of high-energy guitar playing and singing to an audience of locals and tourists. The better I am, the more tips I get.

It's fun to get tips. Only one of the fellows who plays here actually needs his tips. Poor guy—lives in his van and is a very good, well-equipped musician and singer. I like to listen to him and throw him a few bucks when I make his show.

But my body is seventy-eight. That means that regardless of the energy and general health and activity, it is putting on years.

So I had to get a TURP. Google it if you are curious. It's a surgical procedure. Suffice it to say that men of a certain age have to deal with their prostates. When it gets too difficult to function properly, you get pills or a TURP. I got a TURP...three weeks ago. Now it's a struggle to get my energy up for anything. I lie around like a man who accepts his number as the voice of inexorable doom: Slow down. You're on the way out. Give it up. Stop looking at pretty girls and stop taking advantage of the opportunities you get with them. You are too old. You don't have to lie down and die yet, but get used to the idea. No need to be led away kicking and screaming.

But recovery from a TURP is like all recovery. You get yourself back when it's over.

Perhaps I will pass in my sleep, perhaps on my feet. Not sure I'll be led away kicking and screaming, but I am sure I won't be lying around waiting for it. Pretty girls, watch out.

On my feet until the end.

* * *

As the piece suggests, Bob doesn't feel or act his age. Born in the Bronx, he traveled quite a bit—Pago Pago and American Samoa were his most exotic destinations. Drafted, he did two years in the army, then finished his Masters but didn't use it much. He was married briefly, but it didn't appeal to him; his lovers, he says, were wonderful for the most part, though they were naturally mixed experiences. His employments were not very

planned, regardless of credentials. He just did what felt right in the moment.
    As he continues to do.

Who Ever Heard of a Senior Standup Comic?
Sharon Love Cook

Who hasn't wanted to do standup comedy, making the audience laugh so hard they lose control of their bladders? While many have the desire, when it comes to actually climbing onstage, most people will shy away. Yet for those who've attempted it and gotten laughs, there's no better feeling.

My journey began when I spotted a flyer on a bulletin board at our local community college. It advertised an upcoming comedy course. The message read: **Are you funny? Do you like to make people laugh?** I nodded to myself. Although my husband (the sorehead) might not agree, I considered myself a funny person. Not only that, I come from a funny family. Growing up, we showed our affection by pulling pranks on each other. My little brother used to drop salamanders down the back of our mother's dress. Although she didn't think it was funny, we siblings did.

The flyer mentioned the comedy course's teacher, a well-known comic in the Boston area. As I wrote down the information, I stopped to reconsider: I was sixty years old. The members of the class would most certainly be young. Who ever heard of a senior standup comic?

Nonetheless, when it came to comedy, I wasn't exactly a newcomer. Years ago, a male high school friend and I took the plunge, performing at a handful of open mic nights in the Boston 'burbs. Calling ourselves Marital Blitz, we pretended to be a couple whose marriage was a battlefield of bickering and snarky remarks.

Open mic nights are when newcomers take the stage to try out their material. They are welcome, providing they bring at least one ticket-buying person. Thus the audience at these nights tends to be sparse. No matter how much your family supports your dream, they balk at hearing your routine for the fifth time, even if you are buying the tickets.

I'll never know if Marital Blitz would have escaped its suburban roots and made it to Vegas. We ran into trouble early on. One of our skits involved a reference to chicken mogul Frank Perdue (remember him?) In our act, my "husband" says, "The chicks are so wild about me, they call me Frank Perdue." My comeback line was: "No, they call you pecker-head." The venue where we'd performed, a Baptist church basement, told us never to return. I think it was the "pecker-head" that got us banned.

Instead of being discouraged, we used it to our advantage. In our publicity material we didn't hide the fact we were Banned in Boston! That got us open mic nights at local bars. At the same time, we still had to bring a paying audience member. My sister not only got a free ticket, she expected us to settle her bar tab, too.

I was just getting comfortable with our act when my partner got married. His wife, for some reason, didn't like the idea of him spending nights at a bar with another woman. She made him drop out. This left me to perform a two-person act solo, doing both the husband's and the wife's lines. Not even Robin Williams could have pulled that off.

The comedy class instructor was a working comic who'd taught a variety of students, from clam diggers to CEOs, he claimed. Although talent played a role, practice and determination were just as important. "You can't teach a person to be funny," he said, "but you can teach them how to structure and present their funny ideas more effectively."

As the weeks passed, we students began to discover our style. At age sixty, I couldn't realistically be an edgy young comic. Thus I turned to what I called "geezer humor." I found inspiration in "senior wellness" catalogs. You know what I'm talking about. Within its pages you'll find nose-hair clippers, support stockings, raised toilet seats, and over fifty cures for erectile dysfunction.

Although I found such products amusing, my audience, the (young) late-night bar crowd, showed little interest. Not only that, they heckled me. I had no response, other than to mutter "punks!" and rush off the stage.

Before long, graduation night arrived. For our "final exam" we were to perform a five-minute set in front of a dinner theater audience. That entire day I was paralyzed with fear. My pockets bulged with scraps of paper on which I'd scribbled jokes in case my memory failed me. Sitting with my fellow student comics, I wiped my palms on shredded napkins. My family had cheered when I walked in with the class. "Let me not disgrace myself," I prayed.

Finally it was my turn. Walking to the podium, fear turned to anticipation: I had some funny jokes to share! Stepping onstage, I felt the audience's approval. Or maybe it was pity; I was, after all, thirty years older than most students. It also didn't hurt that the audience had had a few cocktails. They laughed at all the right places. Not only did I remember my lines, I ad-libbed. And while my deodorant failed me, my mind stayed the course.

After my closing bow, I strutted offstage. Uppermost in my mind was a single thought: I'm taking this act to Vegas!

* * *

Sharon Love Cook, of Beverly, Massachusetts, is the author of the *Granite Cove Mysteries* and the recent *15 Reasons Why: Men Are for Now, Cats Are Forever*, available at bookstores and online.

There Are Crazies Swimming in the Senior Dating Pool
Arthur Lindower

When I broke up with my last girlfriend a year and a half ago, I considered not dating anymore. I had used online dating in the past and had some success—but I also experienced a lot of disappointment. Women lied to me—often. Some seemed very nice at first but soon were lying about their level of interest. Some had no real interest but used me to buy them dinners and movie or show tickets. Some women rejected me because I wasn't sexually aggressive on our first date, while others did so because they thought a real kiss on our third or fourth date was too aggressive.

My head was spinning, but I finally decided to forge ahead and hoped to meet a mentally stable, nice woman whom I could enjoy being with. Then I met a woman who topped all my other nightmares with online dating.

It started well enough. We hit it off on the phone and had a very nice first date. She offered a very nice kiss at the conclusion of the date, and I gratefully returned the kiss. We went out twice more in a week's time, and we both seemed to thoroughly enjoy our conversations. The dates led us to necking extensively.

On our fourth date, we went to the beach to share some food and drink, and continued to nurture what we both hoped would lead to a full relationship. At this point, we had known each other for two weeks. I offered to pick her up and drive her to the beach, but she declined my offer, saying she would simply meet me at the beach.

    We were there for about ten or fifteen minutes when we kissed, and then she wanted to know when I would see her again. I told her that I had plans for Friday and Saturday with my guy friends, plans we'd made months before. We were going to the racetrack for two special days called the Breeders' Cup, our third year doing this. I'm a serious racing fan.

    She immediately got very upset, asking how could I abandon her on the weekend? I told her I could see her Thursday and Sunday, but she declared this was not acceptable. She started screaming at me, insisting that if I did this, that I would always put friends and family before her. She then bolted down the beach.

    I waited twenty minutes for her to return. But when she did, she again berated me.

    I packed up my stuff and offered to walk her back to her car. I told her I was leaving because of her complete overreaction to the circumstance. She refused to understand my logic and walked away from me. I left.

She called me thirty minutes later. She still didn't like how I'd treated her but said she would see me Sunday. I told her I couldn't see her anymore, which led to her screaming and cursing at me. Asking her to please not call me again, I hung up.

About a month later, after another experience with a crazy person, I said, "Never again." There are too many insane women out there.

But my story has a happy ending.

At that point, I told my chiropractor, Dr. Jason Cleveland, that I was through with online dating. All I wanted was a nice woman who didn't want to get married and didn't want to live together.

Two days later, Doc Jason asked me if I had been serious in what I'd said to him. I said yes. He told me that after speaking to me he'd had a conversation with an old friend who said she was ready to get a boyfriend. He asked her what she wanted, and she said she was looking for a nice guy who didn't want to get married or live together.

Bingo!

He asked me if I was interested. I said yes. I called her, and we've been together over a year now. Maybe Doc Jason needs to add "matchmaker" to the lettering on his storefront office window. I saw him for chiropractic work but wound up with a girlfriend.

All's well that ends well!

* * *

Arthur Lindower is a retired advertising sales manager for one of New York's daily papers and now lives in South Florida, where he enjoys his family, travelling, sports, and attending horse-racing. Arthur used to own a piece of several horse-owner partnerships but now just goes to the track with no vested interest in who wins beyond the $2 win tickets he has purchased. His kids and grandkids are the absolute center of his adoration, but his girlfriend runs a close second.

Bees in the Bonnet and Birds Among the Hats
Erika Hoffman

I went to get a haircut today. It had been a while. Christmas was coming. A few jpgs might get snapped on the twenty-fifth. Anyway, Tonya greeted with me with the usual perfunctory question all hairdressers ask if they haven't seen you in a while: "How've you been?"

In the next ten minutes, she was sure to regret those words.

"Well, for starters, two weeks ago I slipped on wet leaves on a slick boat deck and thought I'd broken my leg. I wanted to vomit, after I stopped seeing stars. I banged up my shin. See." I lifted my pantleg.

"You did," she agreed while gazing at my black-and-blue, still slightly swollen limb.

"Could have been worse." I shrugged. "A thin woman would have broken a hip."

"Well, aside from that, how have you been?"

"My son in Greensboro asked me to babysit for a weekend. While I was at his house, a huge snowstorm hit, and two days turned into four. Besides my redheaded grandson's 'terrible twos' tantrums, my son and his wife had just brought home two puppies—Golden Retrievers. I had trouble catching them, after I put them out to do their business. I was afraid I'd fall again— on their frozen deck."

"You got home okay?"

"After four long days, with a cold and a cough—compliments of daycare."

"Sounds like you've been through it lately."

"Today took the cake. I got up to fix breakfast for my husband before he left for work. While making omelets, I kept hearing a chirping sound near our cabinets where our glasses are stored."

"A bird?" Tonya snipped away at my limp hair.

"All week long I'd complained of a draft. When my husband came down the stairs, he heard the peep-peeping too. So, he checked the flue to the fireplace in the den. It was open. Once before, a bird had gotten into our home. 'Remember?' I queried him. 'That bird was hard to catch!' He peered up at our cathedral ceilings. On top of those kitchen cabinets, I keep a hat collection with his grandma's pinned hats, cowboy hats, a racoon hat, a small yarmulke from a trip to Israel a son had once taken, a policeman's hat, and an old-fashioned hexagon hatbox. Other women might display artificial, silk, tropical flowers atop their cabinets, but they only collect dust. Me, I display hats—which collect dust."

"Was the bird up there?"

"My husband's a pretty big guy, and—like me—not young. He retrieved a stepstool from the pantry, and after mounting it, he climbed onto the countertop below the glass cabinets. This stone countertop's filled with letters, bills, magazines, books, and a few of the grandchildren's toys."

She began blowing my hair.

"'Be careful!' I warned him. 'You don't want to slip on a glossy magazine cover and fall.' I could never stand like that. 'You have pretty good balance for an old guy,' I encouraged.

"He picked up each hat and looked under, but no bird. When he descended to the countertop, the chirping ended; a few of the disturbed papers fluttered off.

"'It's got to be up there still,' I said. 'Did you look behind the mannequin torso with the cowboy vest in the corner?' So my obedient husband once again mounted the stepstool, climbed up on the counter, stood erect at 5'10, and tried to lift the mannequin.

"'Still no bird,' he announced. Then he squatted down and stepped onto the stepstool, and a few more papers dislodged from our hoarders' mess on our countertop.

"Suddenly, I heard a dog bark —from the same direction as the peeping."

"'Those aren't our dogs?' he asked."

"'No. Was that a pig oinking?' I inquired. My husband looked completely baffled. I went over to the countertop and shuffled the piles around, and then I heard a horse neigh after something clattered to the kitchen floor from the mounded pile."

Tonya stopped curling my hair a minute and looked perplexed.

"I picked up a rectangular wooden puzzle called 'A Sound Puzzle/Pets by Melissa and Doug' with the caption 'Crafted by hand.' On this wooden board were animal cut-outs, and if you picked an animal shape up by a small red tack, the animal blurted out its distinguishing sound, be it a cat's meow, a dog's bark, a frog's croak, a sheep's bleat, a parrot's squawk, or a mouse's chirp."

I told her how I'd laughed then and commented to my husband— with beads of sweat on his brow after the stair-stepping routine he'd completed this morning before breakfast—that it's a lucky thing he hadn't fallen because it would be difficult to explain to the EMS why a man of a certain age was up on top of high counters looking atop even higher glass cabinets for an imaginary bird that we could only hear but not see. They'd have thought he was hallucinating, and his crazy old wife was gaslighting him by seconding his claim.

My hair was done. Her next customer awaited. I gave her a large tip. After all, it was the week before Christmas, and she was a captive audience to whom I had enjoyed telling my bird-in-the-hat story. Before I departed, Tonya said, "Always enjoy your stories, Erika."

"Me too. By the way, my hair looks great."

Who knows? It might have just been the movement of us walking past that jiggled the floorboards and in turn jiggled the puzzle.

* * *

Erika Hoffman mostly pens inspirational, non-fiction essays that appear in anthologies such as *Chicken Soup for the Soul* or in regional magazines like *Sasee* of Myrtle Beach. She's had her advice on writing humor appear in *The Writer* as well as having her essays on the craft published in the online *Funds for Writers* magazine. Monthly, she pens a column on the subject of writing for the section called The Writers' Table in the ezine *Page & Spine.* Additionally, she teaches a course for Olli at Duke University on composing the personal essay. Although her niche seems to be the non-fiction narrative, she's crafted fictional stories that have been featured in *Deadly Ink Anthologies, Tough Lit. Magazines*, and *Page & Spine.* In toto, she's had 220 pieces published and has been paid for most of them. Most recently, in March of 2019, Library Partners Press of Wake Forest University published her mystery, *Why Mama.*

    Erika taught public high school for ten years and raised four children. Her degrees are from Duke University. She and her husband reside in Chapel Hill, North Carolina.

OMG, SMH, and IDGAF
Mark T. Holmes

As the years pile on, I find myself to be even less of a drinker than I was in my younger days, and I was setting no bar tab records back then. I've never been the brightest bulb in the box, but I can be something of a quick study. It only took me getting stone drunk three times over the course of ten years to see the light of moderation. As a nineteen-year-old Coast Guard radioman-wannabe working on my months-long training on Governors Island in the middle of New York Harbor, I had the opportunity to partake in ten-cent beer night at the base bowling alley. One dollar's worth of Schlitz later, my head was spinning, first clockwise, then counterclockwise, and having stumbled my way back to the barracks, I loudly announced my intention to all passersby never to drink again. With seven plus more years to go in the service, you can guess the extent to which that promise was kept.

There's a certain amount of peer pressure while bar-hopping in Key West on an overnight liberty during an otherwise boring patrol in the Gulfstream. So, a year after bowling with my brain, once again, I bowed to the moment and found myself being carded (I was way underage) at Sloppy Joe's despite having downed a few beers earlier in the evening at that very location.

We started the evening at Sloppy Joe's, worked our way up and back down Duval street, but someone, probably a kind savior, kept me from further spoiling my evening. Given the late hour, I elected to stumble back to my beloved USCGC *Courageous*, tied up at the pier behind its twin sister, the USCGC *Diligence*. At 0300 (3 a.m. on your civilian clocks), one cutter pretty much looked like the other, so I clambered aboard the nearest one, disrupting the sound sleep of the man who was asleep in "my" rack, on the *Diligence*. It only got worse from there as a few hours later, we set sail. That evening proved to be strike two against my on-again, off-again drinking habits.

After having served eight years and having taken a civilian job for a local savings and loan upon leaving the Coast Guard, I left the company Christmas party completely incapable of driving, and yet foolishly, I did, aiming my car down US 1 with my head out the window, praying to make it home, much less not be thrown in jail. I knew it was going to be a rough night as I watched one of our mortgage underwriters dumping an enormous bottle of vodka into the punch bowl. And that was my final act of alcoholic stupidity, some forty years ago. It wasn't my final act of stupidity, just my final act of the alcoholic kind.

These days, working on my sixty-eighth trip around the sun, there's dust on the few remaining bottles in my cabinet bar, and if I do tread there, it's merely for one drink. I just don't like what the fermented liquid does to my body, an increasingly frail sleeve that seems determined to get me back for past indiscretions at every opportunity.

However....

On a recent cruise that included a day-long stop in Cozumel, I was introduced to and seduced by a super-premium tequila not available in the U.S. I fell for the marketing pitch and the oh-so-smooth, velvety drink that slid ever so seductively down my throat. One hundred dollars later, I boarded the tour bus back to the ship, carefully cradling my Regalo de Dios (gift of God) Extra Anejo bottle of precious tequila. I had gotten drunk again; not on the liquid itself, but on the marketing pitch. I don't regret it, much, and once in a while, I'll reach for that expensive, super-premium tequila and with that particular visit or other cruises in mind, think back to the joy and beauty of traversing foaming azure seas while on patrols on the *Courageous*, partaking in sometimes desperate rescues, hanging over the bow as dolphins leapt and danced in front of us, and marveling at a billion stars in the night sky as we rolled over and through the waves and troughs of the great Atlantic Ocean.

I have two gym memberships and pay for neither one. Thank you, Silver Sneakers, for buoying my often-vain efforts at getting enough exercise so that I don't simply collapse in a miserable heap of sinew and fat. The gym with the pretty young women in yoga pants and ponytails is but a mile from my house. Retro Fitness has tons of equipment, free weights, and everything you need to throw out your back. The pretty young women are usually being pestered by the guys with the thigh-like biceps, who drive the huge pickup trucks that take up two precious parking spaces and who must, I imagine, down handfuls of supplements daily. So I don't go there. I go to the JCC, home to my contemporaries: older guys and women who are clinging to some semblance of well-being and not particularly concerned with impressing anyone. There are no huge, black pickup trucks in the JCC lot, just Toyota sedans, a few SUVs, and the occasional Buick with the half-landau padded roof and aftermarket hood ornament. My kind of folks. Did I just admit to that? OMG.

    A trip to the grocery store is increasingly like a college entrance exam. There's a lot of reading of ingredients, on-the-spot calculating of calories and especially fiber content, plus the inevitable mathematics of predicting the final bill. Some of the stuff we enjoy eating comes home only on BOGO days. Not that it's good for me, but I like an English muffin now and then—however, when the individual package sells for north of four dollars, uh-uh. When the store puts them on buy one get one, home they come, one in the freezer, one in the bread bin.

I'm not a very patient shopper, unlike my wife, who fancies a trip to the market like a royal retreat with the queen herself. Hours go by, and I wonder where she is. She relishes the experience; I am a strategic hit-and-run shopper. Her way is startlingly more efficient when it comes to price because she actually shops, while I'm limited by my maleness to simply buying. I didn't write the book *See It, Want It, Buy It*, but I certainly could have.

The biggest issue in shopping for groceries is that none of the stuff you really should be buying, the stuff that's good for you, is ever on the BOGO list. It's always the processed food, the canned stuff made by people who apparently own salt mines, and snacks that contain artery-collapsing amounts of saturated fat that are normally on BOGO. However, in deference to saving money, or so we think, we do ferret out enough reasonably healthy BOGO choices to make it worthwhile: sauces, Heinz ketchup (it's a vegetable, right?), and the occasional box of whole-grain pasta.

We have many of those. Contrary to some opinions, it does not taste like the box it came in. Not even close. Trust me. I say, give me a BOGO on the baby spinach, queen olives, nuts, lentils, hummus, and salad fixings that I truly need. If you see that kind of BOGO, come find me at the gym. You know, the one with no pickups in the parking lot.

    My outlook on doctors and dentistry has always been in the realm of hate-hate. I grew up getting fillings without Novocain. Long story; creeps me out to even think about it, so use your imagination. I was moved closer to the hate-hate outlook one time twenty years ago or so when I was dispatched to a dental specialist by my regular dentist (a wonderful woman whom I trust very much). When I checked in to the palatial office and presented my insurance card (I was gainfully and corporately employed at the time), the receptionist lit up like the Fourth of July and exclaimed, "Oooh! You have great insurance!" I thought I heard a cash register chime. The only thing missing was one of those bells they have at the bar at Fridays. You know, the one they ring when a great tip is left, or someone chugs an entire pitcher of Schlitz.

    I was then escorted to a room that must have been created by NASA, with a rotating, full-head, super-duper digital X-ray machine that must cost a thousand dollars just to turn on the power switch. I obediently kept my head very still on the probably unsanitized chin rest while this "thing" encircled my cranium, pumping me with untold roentgens of head-glowing radiation. I don't recall whatever the treatment was, but I'll bet it was uncomfortable.

I have seven or eight dental crowns, and I've stopped counting. I was getting gold crowns for durability, but when gold spiked in price, we went back to porcelain. I never did get my grille and have only two molar gold crowns left. When one needs the inevitable replacement, guess who's keeping the old one?

With this many years on the planet, I've seen enough advances and retreats in health and medicine to know that a lot of these experts truly are guessing. Eat eggs. Don't eat eggs. Butter is bad for you; eat margarine. Forget margarine; go back to butter. Everyone needs a colonoscopy. Okay, not everyone. We've got one out of every thousand colonoscopies ending up with a perforated bowel. Maybe a lot of you only need a sigmoidoscopy. Yeah, that's it. You need glaucoma medicine, and...oh, sorry, it's not covered by your laughably inadequate yet super-expensive insurance. That cost will have to come out of your $7000 deductible. Thanks. Two years later: Oh wait, you didn't need glaucoma medicine after all. Sorry.

The point is, too much of medicine, and especially pharmaceuticals, is about money first, doctors second, and patients somewhere down the list. We have become pincushions for Medicare, and I'm not having it. My older friend Al remarked one time over dinner how his new doctor had him lined up for every test under the sun. Al had supplemental insurance, so he cared not about the out-of-pocket price; his monthly payment covered basically everything. How many of those tests were needed? I'll wager that most of them were of the optional variety, but since the doctor's office had a "live one" with great coverage, do 'em all. Of course, all these expensive tests turned up nothing, but a lot of people got paid a lot of money.

Somehow, our generation has raised up the likes of Martin Shkreli, the so-called "pharma bro," who is now someone else's "bro" in prison. As you know, he was the flag-bearer for out-of-control pharmaceutical prices, having driven up the price of Daraprim from $13 to $750 a pill, among his other misdeeds. Sadly, this felon is not alone in ripping off American consumers. The goal, it would seem, is to separate all of us from all our money up to and beyond the grave. For this, the above reasons, and many more, my hate-hate relationship with the industry endures. It is among the most bitter "pills" to swallow in seniorhood, and one that members of our own generation and the one we raised have laid upon us. There is no savior on the horizon, so eat the veggies and go to the JCC.

I joined AARP the moment I was eligible. That was a benefit I'd earned by surviving thus far, and I wanted my damned dollar off at the Lowery Zoo, my first use of the age-based discount. My biggest issue with senior discounts, though, is that I virtually never remember to ask for them, and a surprisingly large number of establishments keep it a dark secret. Somewhere in the back of my brain I know that Publix, our supermarket, gives a five percent discount to seniors on Wednesdays, but do they look at you and say, "Here ya go," or do they wait for you to ask for it? You're correct. Like everywhere else, you must know it exists, and you must ask.

I'd think the management would want you to love their store even more and have the cashiers look at you and make a judgment, or at least ask for your ID or the year you were born. Wouldn't you just love that store? Wouldn't you go back there like spawning salmon up the Columbia River? Of course, you would, and you'd tell all your condo buddies, your sister in Naples, and the neighbor who sometimes speaks to you, but it just doesn't happen. In response, I'll leave you with another acronym I learned online: SMH.

Time is a-wasting. Go for that walk. Feed the birds. Write your book. Go on a vacation and spend some of that money you're hoarding. Above all, be well.

* * *

Mark T. Holmes is a commercial writer and former marketing executive for large banks and credit unions. Following a layoff from a lucrative senior marketing job at one of the nation's largest credit unions during the past recession, Mr. Holmes formed his own Florida S-corporation, Idea Depot, Inc., and began writing high-end military transition and executive federal resumes, along with doing web development and optimization work gaining page one results, plus marketing writing for a message-on-hold company.
In 2014, Mr. Holmes released his first book, *Streams to Ford*, a book of poetry long in the making, followed in 2015 by *Always Ready— Coast Guard Sea Stories from the 1970s,* and in 2016, the World War II novel, *Artifact - A B-24 Crew, a British Spy, and Churchill's Deadly Obsession.* All books are available in print and Kindle format on Amazon.

Mark and his wife, Sheri, operate a retail location in an antique mall and trade in antiques and vintage cameras in the store and online.

Across the Vast Divide
Ann Favreau

It was in the Hakone region of Japan, as I made my way up the uneven stone steps toward the summit, where the hot springs far below could be viewed, that I knew that I had stepped on the other side of young. My legs refused to carry me beyond midway. My throat closed up with the sulfurous smell, and I started to cough. My heart pounded in my chest. Reluctantly, I turned around and headed down. My eyes watched carefully to avoid a misstep as I descended.

Since the symptoms disappeared as the air became clearer, I chalked the experience up to the toxic environment and jet lag. However, what became apparent as I boarded the tram that would take us high in the air across the mountainous area above the hot springs below was that my steps of youth were no more. They had been replaced with the vagaries of age. This unexpected manifestation surprised me. I didn't feel old. I didn't have daily aches and pains. My mind was active. I still had a sense of adventure. Well, of course—here I was in Japan, experiencing a new land and a new culture. However, my muscles had betrayed me on this climb.

Was this just an aberrant occurrence or the clarion call for things to come? Had I crossed some invisible great divide from youth to old age? Looking back, I had hopscotched through childhood, playing games and moving with fluidity. In college I surprised myself with the stamina for field hockey and a killer volleyball serve. As a young mother, I was a whirlwind of energy from dawn to late night. As a kindergarten teacher, I was on the go all day, bending, stretching, stooping, getting up and sitting down on little chairs to interact with young children.

    Cancer, retirement, and an errant thyroid gland brought on a more sedentary existence. Though the years were accumulating, I still considered myself young. Would I let this fleeting travel experience change my view of life? Perhaps, but I would view the crossover from youth to old age like this silent tram ride between the mountains with the hot springs of experience bubbling beneath. It would be a quiet transition, acknowledged, but without a negative impact on my state of mind. I would continue to see myself as young at heart.

* * *

Ann Favreau is a vibrant eighty-one-year-old retired educator, who lives in Venice, Florida. She is a member of the Florida Writers Association and past president of the Suncoast Writers Guild, Inc. Her writing has been published in many newspapers, magazines, anthologies, and ezines. She has won local and national prizes for her prose and poetry. She is a thirty-one-year colorectal cancer survivor and a member of the National Colorectal Cancer Roundtable. Her most recent book, *It's Okay to Have an Ostomy,* is available on Amazon.com. Currently she is president of the Friends of Ostomates Worldwide-USA, a national non-profit organization that sends donated ostomy supplies at no cost to ostomates in need in ninety countries around the world. She describes herself as a traveler who marvels at the awesome and finds wonder in the ordinary.

A Day in the Life
Linda Peters

It's early, at least for me. Ken has been up for hours already. I yawn and stretch lazily in the bed, roll onto my side, and debate whether to go back to sleep or get up.

My mind is made up for me when Ken comes into the bedroom, his cane rapping hard on the floor, a sound I know he hopes will wake me. I roll over and glare at him.

"Oh, did I wake you?" he says while trying to look innocent. As if after forty years I didn't know his thoughts as well as my own. I consider throwing my pillow at him, but the last time I did that the arthritis in my shoulder flared up and he nearly tripped on his cane and fell. It wasn't worth it. So I get up.

"Well," he says, "as long as you're getting up, how's about some breakfast? I'm starving."

I mutter something under my breath, something that will surely need to be cleaned out with mouthwash, and get dressed.

The thing is, Ken is the cook around here. At least, he used to be. He has the touch, the innate ability to cook without measuring or reading recipes. His food is always better than mine. But now, ever since he hurt his leg when he fell off the porch, he wants me to do everything for him. We could argue all day over who is worse off—him with his hearing problems and cane, or me with my arthritis and digestion problems. Still, we've loved each other for four decades. We must be doing something right.

Once my mouth is thoroughly cleansed of impure thoughts, I shuffle to the living room, where Ken is snoring in his recliner with the remote dangling off the ends of his fingers. This is his morning routine. I snatch the remote and he immediately wakes. "I was watching that," he says.

"Then you can see through your eyelids," I reply. "So what do you want for breakfast?"

"I don't know."

"Well, tell me something."

"I don't care. Whatever you want to fix."

"Cereal."

"What?"

"Cereal."

"You call that breakfast? No."

"How about pancakes and sausage?"

"Huh?"

I sigh. "Pan-cakes and sau-sage."

"Uh-uh."

"Oatmeal?"

"Naw. Doesn't sound right."

"Eggs, then."

"Legs? Don't want no chicken for breakfast."

"No, Ken. Eggs."

"Beg? I don't beg for nothin'."

"EGGS, KEN, EGGS. Put your hearing aids in!"

He mutters, probably saying the same things I muttered earlier. But he puts his "ears" in.

"So, Ken, do you want some eggs?"

"Naw. We had eggs yesterday. Don't want them again."

"Well then, what do you want?"

"I don't care. Anything."

So we have oatmeal with raisins and cinnamon, and toast. I give him the glare that he knows means don't say a word. So he doesn't. Not so dumb after all. But he puts on his pouty face all through breakfast.

After I put the dishes in the dishwasher, I settle on the couch next to Ken's recliner and pick up the yarn and needles I'm using to make a blanket for my future great-grandbaby. The whole family is so excited. Ken tries to hide it by grumbling, but everyone thinks he is just being himself and pays him no attention. I read the instructions for the next five rows but can't quite make out the wording.

"Ken," I say, leaning over and holding the paper where he can see it. "What does it say to do for Rows 5 through 10?"

He grabs the paper from my hand and holds it close and then farther away. "I don't know what language this is, Linda. It must be foreign, though."

I frown. "I don't think so. I've been reading it so far."

He squints. "What words are spelled DC and HDC with asterisks beside them?" He tosses the paper back to me. "Makes no sense to me. You'll have to read it yourself."

I narrow my eyes and strain to see the words. "Why are they making print so much smaller these days? I need a magnifying glass to see anything."

"So put your glasses on, woman."

"I've lost them again."

"Did you check the top of your head?"

I reach up and pat my hair. "They're not up there."

He sighs. "All right. I guess I'll have to find them for you—again."

After a lot of muttering and cane rapping through the house, he comes back into the living room with my glasses.

"Where did you find them?"

"Top shelf of the refrigerator."

"What? Why would they be in there?"

He settles heavily into his chair. "You tell me."

I think hard. Am I losing my mind? Am I steps away from being put in a home? Then I remember. I was trying to read the label on the milk jug to see if it was past the expiration date. It was, so I poured it out in the sink and shut the refrigerator. I must have set my glasses on the shelf while I removed the jug.

Through the years, Ken has found a lot of things I've lost. I've come to rely on him for that. If not for him, I wouldn't know where anything was. Our kids and grandkids may have all kinds of electronic doodads to chime or play music to help them find what they are looking for, but there's nothing manmade that can compare to my Ken's masterful locating skills. As I sit here, reading my pattern, I feel safe. Comfortable. I put down my needles and go to the kitchen, returning with a bowl of homemade peach cobbler. I give it to Ken with a kiss on his forehead.

"I love you," I say.

He frowns. "What do you want to do?" Then he laughs. "I love you too, sweetie. Always have, always will."

* * *

Linda Peters is an avid reader of many genres and enjoys writing stories with satisfying endings. Her story "Blankets of Love" was recently published in *Chicken Soup for the Soul – Volunteering and Giving Back.* Her short story "Unexpected" is included in the Chattanooga Writers' Guild 2018 Anthology.

As the local coordinator for the non-profit Project Linus, she has been featured on *Friday's Hero* by the ABC affiliate in Chattanooga, Tennessee. She has been interviewed on television on several occasions and has had two write-ups in the local newspaper.

Linda has two children, four grandchildren, one great-granddaughter, and one husband. Her current dream is to write a story about Hawaii so she can justify going there on a research trip.

Looking Back from Ninety-One
Dan Samuelson

Is ninety-one old enough for you? I think I qualify as a senior!

The biggest negative of my senior life was the loss of my son at age sixty-six. It's unfair to outlive your children. The upside is he left me a small fortune (and some for my first wife, too), so we're comfortable now because of him. But there is another downside to that: There isn't much we can do to enjoy the money, because my second wife has a lack of mobility due to swollen legs, which I have to wrap for compression every day.

I built a step thing for her that she uses to get in and out of the car, and other places as well. She steps up on it, then gets into the car, and I put it in the back of the car till we arrive at our destination, at which point she uses it to get out. Everywhere we go, she uses the step to get in and out of "the chariot."

Yes, I still drive at ninety-one. I walk with a cane; I guess I drive better than I walk!

We drove up to North Carolina recently. I wanted to see my granddaughter graduate from college. But we got a late start and were still 300 miles from where the ceremony was being held when it was about to start. My son, on the phone, said, "Turn around and go home. You can't possibly make it in time. Besides, you shouldn't be driving at your age anyhow."

Home? Home my foot! Now that we were in the car and on the road, we wanted to go places and see things. So we went to Cape Canaveral and saw a lot of other interesting sights as well, and we went to a lot of restaurants and had good food. We were on the road ten days. We enjoyed it very much except for my missing my two weekly chiropractor appointments. I suffered as a result of missing them.

We want to take a trip down the Rhine River, but I can hardly bring the step with us!

Although it's difficult for my wife to get around, we do sometimes eat out when we're at home. My wife can't cook anymore because of her physical situation, so I do most of the cooking, unless we go to a restaurant—which we did a few times recently. I was cleaning out the fridge the other evening and found all the leftovers from the last three days of restaurant food. I knew we weren't going to eat them, so I threw them out. What a waste!

We live a pretty simple lifestyle. We're certainly not out dancing! We're not involved socially except with our close neighbors, so we watch a lot of TV. Why is it that every show has someone shooting someone else? Our biggest complaint is that everyone is killing everyone else on TV. We much prefer shows that offer singing and dancing, but there aren't that many of those. It's mostly people with guns, firing them off and killing people.

During the day I suppose there are soap operas on TV, but my wife doesn't care for those either, so she spends most of the day sleeping. I guess nobody is shooting anyone else in her dreams, although I don't know if they're singing and dancing, either.

Our biggest joy is our little dog, Heidi.

I led an interesting life in the past. I had a shipyard; I was a tugboat captain; I was a diver for a shipyard; I raced catamarans and sailboats in regattas; I've gone SCUBA diving and sport diving. I've been in some aspect or another of the boat business all of my life. I spent thirty days on the Mediterranean. I also got in 1000 hours of flight time as a pilot. I've had so many interesting experiences. Now my biggest trip is to the chiropractor's office. I'm retired now, but I'm still working: Taking care of my wife and the house is a full-time job.

I enjoy my wife immensely, although she does holler every once in a while. Because of our physical limitations, we're not sexually active any longer, but we still enjoy each other. During my life I have been with some beautiful women, but this marriage has lasted thirty-some-odd years, and my wife is my queen.

* * *

Dan Samuelson is retired from any number of occupations, most of them to do with the water. At ninety-one he still "has all his marbles" and a sense of humor besides. He and his wife live in South Florida, where her physical limitations prevent them from enjoying the local attractions and restaurants as much as they'd like, but fortunately they still very much enjoy each other.

Cleavage Connection
Bobbie Christmas

The year was 2011, and at age sixty-seven I'd been working on losing weight for the hundredth time in my life. At that time I was blogging about my food plan and intentions to lose weight, and the process was working for me. I dropped 60 unwanted pounds.

When I was nearing my lowest weight on that plan, I was working out regularly as well as watching my food intake. After a particularly stringent workout one day, I prepared for my reward: a soak in the hot, aerated spa at the gym. I pulled an old bathing suit out of the bottom of my gym bag. I hadn't worn it in ages, because it had always been tight on me. That day not only did it fit well, but it also emphasized my boobs by pulling them together and showing a little cleavage through an open panel down the front. I laughed at my image, because I usually had what my brother-in-law called "clea," not enough to be considered cleavage.

I thought about a book I was reading about how differently the sexes think. It emphasized that men are wired to size up a woman by her appearance, no matter how much we women may protest that we want to be loved for our brains and our character. Men see large boobs, small noses, a good hips-to-waist ratio, and shapely legs as the most important attributes a woman can have. I looked in the mirror at my body. Ha! I still had almost no waist; I'd always looked more like a fireplug than an hourglass. In the mirror I could see my Jewish nose, cottage-cheese thighs, and boobs that were farther apart than the two sides on the Middle East peace talks, but at least that old, faded, formerly too-small suit smashed my boobs together and gave me cleavage. I sighed and thanked elastic for the assistance. I wasn't on my way to a fashion show; I was on my way to swim and then soak in the hot tub.

    In the pool I swam for twenty minutes without taking a break, but when I glanced over at the hot tub, my usual reward for being a good girl and working out, four men were in it having a lively conversation. I decided to wait them out. My ideal situation was to have the hot tub to myself so I could back up to the strong jets and meditate while I enjoyed a quiet bubble massage. I didn't want to hear those men's conversation or get involved in it. Conversation wasn't easy over the noise of the jets, and I preferred to be silent and relax after a workout. To wait out the males, I stayed in the pool and performed water aerobic exercises for another ten minutes. At last three of the men left the hot tub. I figured the fourth wouldn't be far behind, so I waddled my sixty-seven-year-old fireplug-shaped, cottage-cheese-riddled body over to the hot tub for my reward and quiet time.

The remaining guy nodded recognition of my presence when I slid into the hot water. I nodded back but otherwise ignored him and went to my favorite spot in front of one of the strongest jets in the pool. I closed my eyes and released an uninhibited sigh of relief as the frothy water rolled up my back like warm fingers kneading my overworked muscles.

Over the sound of the bubble jets the guy said, "Feels good, don't it?"

"Yes, almost like a massage," I agreed. I opened my eyes. He wasn't looking at my face. He was looking at my cleavage. Men!

Still staring lower than my chin, he asked, "Would you like a real massage?" [Man talk for "I'd love to get my hands on those tits."]

I glanced at him again: muscled and fit, probably in his late forties, early fifties, with a large but faded tattoo on his arm of a dog holding heavy dumbbells. Apparently he had been lifting weights for years.

Because we were sitting on a submerged bench, the water hit us both at nipple height. His chest was smooth, tight, and hairless, the way I like a man's chest, and he had a tan, even though it was early February. His eyes twinkled, and he had a charming smile, but all those physical attributes were canceled out by the fact that he had said "Feels good, don't it?" I can't tolerate poor English. Women!

What a quandary! The man had offered me a free massage. I love massages, and with his strong muscles, he would probably give me a good strong massage, but should I say yes to a complete stranger, and in a hot tub? My mind went a mile a minute. First, I felt flattered; so few men flirt with a woman who is overweight and in her sixties. I had evolved, worked on my body, improved it a great deal, even if I had much further to go, and as a result, a man was flirting with me. Yes, I felt flattered. Next, though, I felt insulted. He had no interest in my mental acuity, my character, my skills as an editor, or my accomplishments as an entrepreneur. All he could see was my cleavage, which took precedence over all else, and it was falsely created by wearing a suit with a peek-a-boo panel. Last, I felt a little afraid. What if I let him rub my shoulders? Would his hands stray to my cleavage? That's all he seemed interested in, anyway, and what would I do then? No one else was around. How should I respond? I answered in an indirect way and said, "A massage sounds great, but I don't think that's a part of what this gym has to offer." [Woman talk for "I'm saying no, but in a way that won't offend you."]

    He grinned, dropped his head, and coyly looked up at me through his dark blond eyelashes, but he didn't pursue the issue. Instead he asked, "Do you work out with anybody?" [Man talk for "Are you available?"]

"I usually come alone, although I sometimes join friends," I answered. "I'm used to doing things alone." [Woman talk for "Yes, I'm available."] I'm human; I couldn't resist his flirtations completely.

"I saw you swimming. I swam for twelve years when I hurt my back and couldn't lift weights, but I'm better now." [Man talk for "I'm virile and ready to stand at stud."]

"I noticed your tattoos. You must be a weightlifter." [Woman talk for "Yes, I can see that you are virile and strong."]

He lifted his well-endowed bicep and pointed to the image of a vicious-looking dog. "Yeah, I've had this tattoo so long the dog's turned into a poodle." [Man talk for "I'm old enough for you, babe, and I can be gentle, like a poodle."]

I responded, "Hey, I have a poodle, and when you have a poodle, you're never alone." [Woman talk for "Love me, love my dog."]

"I like dogs." [Man talk for "I'll tolerate your little yap-yap if it gets me what I want."] He giggled and added, "I don't know what happened, but since you walked into this hot tub, my shorts started acting up." [Man talk for "I have gotten an erection from looking at your breasts."]

I answered. "My suit fills with air, too." [Woman talk for "I don't want to know about your erection; keep that information to yourself."]

He blatantly glared at my bosom, grinned sheepishly, and said, "Those ain't air. I can tell they're real." [Man talk for exactly what he said, without any regard for or knowledge of the fact that he has insulted the woman.] He then stood, raising his body out of the water and displaying the vast difference between the broad width of his shoulders and the narrowness of his waist. [The male display/mating dance.] He adjusted his waistband and sat back down.

Although shocked that he would say something so blatant about my boobs, I laughed inwardly at what turned out to be a typical male. After his display, if I stood, he'd see that I had almost no waistline. He'd see the blubbered Bobbie probably old enough to be his mother. I didn't stand. [The female attempt at hiding anything that isn't an asset.]

We talked a little more; I learned he was a bricklayer, which explained the tan. He learned almost nothing about me; men fail to ask personal questions when their focus is strictly on the physical. He finally rose and left the hot tub, saying he enjoyed talking to me.

I leaned back, closed my eyes again, and relaxed into the harmless bubble massage I had earned.

***

Bobbie Christmas, a writer and editor who lives in Georgia, has been single most of her life. She founded Zebra Communications, a book-editing firm, in 1992, and it is still going strong. In her senior years she has enjoyed writing about her odd, awkward, and funny experiences in the dating world.

www.ingramcontent.com/pod-product-compliance
Lightning Source LLC
Chambersburg PA
CBHW031155020426
42333CB00013B/682